Note This book is dedicated to all of those who have
lost someone tragically and to the following:

to Mary who was the inspiration for the book; to Dr. Art
Arauzo who gave me the courage to write this book; and to
Peg Hamilton, an english teacher for editing the book.

TO MARY

I WILL LOVE YOU TODAY MORE THAN
I LOVED YOU YESTERDAY

I WILL LOVE YOU TOMORROW MORE
THAN I LOVE YOU TODAY

MIKE

A True Love Story
A Second Chance at Love

Michael Van Buren Latch

Order this book online at www.trafford.com
or email orders@trafford.com

Most Trafford titles are also available at major online book retailers.

Printed in the United States of America.

ISBN: 978-1-4269-2890-1 (sc)
ISBN: 978-1-4269-2891-8 (hc)
ISBN: 978-1-4269-2997-7 (e)

Library of Congress Control Number: 2010903511

Trafford rev. 7/19/2010

 www.trafford.com

North America & international
toll-free: 1 888 232 4444 (USA & Canada)
phone: 250 383 6864 ♦ fax: 812 355 4082

Chapter One

The story begins in the fall of 1979 when I was looking forward to my senior year. I had arrived in Oxford with my best friend Ronnie, and we had decided to rent an apartment at Jackson Square, an apartment complex about five miles from the campus of The University of Mississippi, which everyone calls Ole Miss! Not a care in the world for these two best friends who had known one another since they were five years old.

We were on the same Little League team, the Bears, to start with at age five. Competed against one another in The Don Blasingame League, me on the Rotary and Ronnie on the Kiwanis, and were teammates again in the Junior Y League, the Birds. Ronnie was the brother that I never had and here we were about to embark on our final year of college. We had decided that we were going to have fun and do it up right.

Ronnie and I had initially gone to Ole Miss to play baseball. We had known each other for the past twelve years. We were seventeen when we enrolled at Ole Miss, and we were ready to conquer the world and make it all the way to the major leagues.

I was a month and a day older than Ronnie and always teased him about being older than he was, especially when I turned eighteen. You see, the drinking age at the time that we entered Ole Miss was eighteen. I became legal on September 21st. I thought that I was a BMOC, Big Man on Campus and ribbed Ronnie about it unmercifully for the next month and a day until Ronnie became legal on October 22nd. This was a time when the pundits considered eighteen to be adulthood. A soldier can fight for his country at eighteen but cannot drink until he/she is twenty one. Where is the justice in that, but I do not want to stray from the story.

Ronnie's dream, as well as my own had always been to play major league baseball. We had been playing since we were five years old, and the both of us had been groomed by our fathers. Ronnie's dad played at Ole Miss back in the fifties and my dad had played baseball in the Army with Willie Mays and Curt Simmons, just to name a few. When my dad was discharged from the Army he pursued baseball in the semi-pro circuit playing for the Corinth Rockets, located in Corinth, Mississippi, until he tore his hamstring and his playing days were over. So it was only natural that two seventeen year old boys, who idolized their fathers, wanted to follow in their footsteps, but take it one step farther, all the way to the "Major League" level.

Unfortunately for me, I hurt my right shoulder, which was my pitching arm. I had been an All-Conference pitcher both my junior and senior year. When I was in high school, for my height, I could throw the baseball really hard. Mark B., another pitcher on our high school team asked the head baseball coach, Johnny Plummer, why I threw so hard and his response was, with tongue in cheek I might add, "Latch farts when he throws." This was far from the truth but Mark, as well as everyone else, got a big laugh out of that.

I injured my shoulder playing touch football on a Sunday afternoon with a bunch of sorority girls along with some football players and baseball players. As for Ronnie, well, he got screwed by the Head Coach because he played favorites. The coach did "not play the best player." He played friends of his who had kids on the team or former alumni's kids. He was in all actuality a complete ASS.

This all happened our freshman year, so needless to say we were both very disappointed. But we both were damned and determined to give it our all our sophomore, year but the circumstances with my shoulder did not afford me the opportunity to realize my college dream much less my major league aspirations. Ronnie was screwed for the second consecutive year, and this made him lose all interest in baseball at that time.

After my sophomore year Ronnie and I thought that it would be good if we both had a change of scenery. Since we both knew a lot of people who were going to Mississippi State, we thought why the HELL not give State a try and see what happens.

The head baseball coach at Ole Miss had put a really bad taste in both our mouths, so the following year we headed to Starkville. We tried to adapt the best way that we could. We played intramural football as well as softball and tried to fit in. The first year was Okay and we decided to go back to State for another year. We had to adapt to new surroundings and a new way of life because there was definitely a difference between Ole Miss and State. I roomed with David and two other guys the first year and then Kirby and Rickey G the second year. To be honest I don't remember who Ronnie roomed with, but I think it was Rickey W.

Now you want to talk about a crazy loon? Then Rickey W. was one! I probably know enough stuff about him to write another book but let's not get off the subject. After the debacle at Starkville, two lost years, Ronnie lost interest in college and I knew beyond a shadow of a doubt what I would be doing the following year; get my "ass" back to Ole Miss!

While I was home during the summer my decision to return to Ole Miss was an easy one and I wanted to see if I could convince Ronnie to re-enroll and get his degree as well. My selling point was that if he had his degree then no one would be able to take it away from him. After much thought about what I had said, Ronnie agreed to return to Ole Miss with me in August of 1979. Little did I know that my life was about to change in a way that I would have never have imagined.

I look back and sometimes I still can't believe that I went to Mississippi State. Not that it was a bad college or anything like that; it's just that it wasn't for me or Ronnie for that matter. But when you are young and your dreams are crushed you do Stupid Things.

Once I returned to Ole Miss I saw that I would need an additional year. The transfer to Mississippi State had put me on the "five year plan", rather than the normal four. No big deal, I thought. I would graduate in 1980 instead of 1979. What's one more year? Enough to change you forever!

You see, I was free as the wind, but what happened to me at a local Sunflower grocery store in Oxford, Mississippi, would blow me over like I never thought was possible. I only thought that I had been in love before, until that day. Yeah, I loved the college life, my family, friends, and baseball, thought that I had been in love in high school. Not in my wildest imagination did I contemplate for one second that a greater love would enter my life during this senior year that would totally blow me away!

Chapter Two

Once I was registered for class and found out who my professors would be, it was time for the final year. Graduate and get a job with the degree that I was about to earn was all that I mattered to Ronnie and me.

Ronnie and I didn't have any classes together for the first time since we had been freshman at Ole Miss back in 1975. Good thing that we didn't since the last time we did Ronnie cost me an A!

You see, we were taking a speech class and I had an A with about three weeks left. We were supposed to give a speech in front of the class, and Ronnie was apprehensive about doing this. He could talk to anyone now, but at that time in his life he did not like to stand up in front of people and pontificate.

I, on the other hand, would stand up in front of the United States Congress or anyone else for that matter and let-it-rip! Hell, I didn't care who was in the audience. If I had something to say then I would say it in a heartbeat. Mouth in gear before brain is running happened more times than I care to remember.

Needless to say Ronnie and I didn't go to class that day and subsequently I went from an A to a B. So much for listening to your best friend when your grade in on the line. This wasn't the first time that I had screwed up and probably would not be the last was what I thought.

Ronnie and I had gone to Ole Miss to locate a place to live earlier before the fall semester. We decided on Jackson Square apartments. These apartments were only a few miles from campus. When we took the tour the apartment was within our budget, and it had what we needed: two bedrooms, a full bath, kitchen, and den that was located on the first floor. This afforded us easy entry and exit, not to mention the move in. No stairs to lug furniture up as well as everything else that two roommates would need.

When we moved into Jackson Square we had no idea that there would be people from our hometown living there as well. They were living across the parking lot from where Ronnie and I were. We knew that we were back where we belonged, and it would be "party time" all semester long.

I also met two guys from Booneville, Mississippi, through some of the classes I was registered for. We became friends almost immediately. They would definitely play a part in what would transpire in the not too distant future. You never know who you may meet that will help or hurt you in your life. These two individuals assisted me on one fateful night.

The first morning of class that fall of 1979, I got up as usual. I showered, shaved, got dressed with my Levi's and button-down Ralph Lauren polo shirt, and then put on my Nike's. Then I reached for my "trademark" visor and put it on. My stomach was growling slightly so I had some Cheerios and out the apartment door I went.

My first class of the day was advertising. I was marketing major, and I thought that this would be a good elective to take. Someone had told me while I was registering that the professor was somewhat easy, so I thought, "Hey, get an easy A or an easy B." That wouldn't hurt the GPA my final year, now would it?

I was on my way to class that morning and noticed that I was out of cigarettes. I stopped at this Sunflower grocery store to buy a pack. It was and still is a very bad habit, but at that time--when you're young--death is something that you never think about, so having a smoke was nothing in my eyes. Hell, everyone I knew was smoking something, if you know what I mean. For me it was cigarettes, and that morning I was out.

I knew there was a Sunflower grocery store not far from where Ronnie and I lived. I had seen it when we drove toward the apartment complex when we were moving in the previous weekend and even commented to Ronnie that it was nice that we were so close to a grocery store.

Ronnie and I had even been in there to buy some groceries and other necessary items on the Saturday that he had arrived. There seemed to be nothing out of the ordinary about this grocery store. It was like all of the Sunflower stores that I had been in previously…canned foods, fresh vegetables, milk, bread, etc. Well, that was Saturday afternoon. It is amazing how things can change within forty-eight hours. That Monday morning when I walked in the Sunflower, the scenery had changed considerably.

When I entered the grocery store that Monday morning my jaw dropped to the floor! At first I thought that I must be dreaming because not ten feet from the entrance, right in front of my eyes, was the most beautiful girl I had ever seen in my life.

She was standing at the cash register keying in the prices. Now remember, this is 1979, and there were no scanners for the bar codes. Everything was done manually, and this girl's fingers were flying over the keys.

She was talking to the little lady who was checking out like she had known her all of her life. This was odd, as I would find out later, because she was originally from California.

I finally got my jaw back off of the floor and thought to myself, "thank God she didn't see my expression." If this "goddess" had seen the way I gawked at her when I first walked in, within the span of about three minutes I would have made a double fool of myself. You remember what I said earlier about there are times that "my mouth starts in motion before my brain was in gear?" Well, it could not have happened at a worse time than when I met the most beautiful girl face to face for the first time.

I eased around the corner so I was the next in line. While I waited I became mesmerized by this girl's beauty. As the little lady was leaving, the most beautiful girl was telling her thanks, to come back soon and have a nice day. Then she turned toward me, smiled, and asked if she could help me?

With her gorgeous smile, and the silkiness of her voice, well I was "TOTALLY SMITTEN"! She could have asked me to jump on one leg; to crawl around the store; do anything and I would have been more than happy to have done what she asked. I would have done it with a smile on my face. She had my heart, my brain, my soul all at one time. All that she had done was smile at me and asked me how she could help me.

It took me a moment to gain my composure. When I had, I proceeded to tell her that I would like a pack of Vantage non-menthol cigarettes. While she was getting the cigarettes, my heart sank when I saw what I considered to be a wedding ring on her left hand.

With me being an Ole Mississippi boy from Corinth, with a bubbly and outgoing personality who had never been at a loss for words. I said, "Nice ring. How long have you been married?" To which she replied, "I'm not married. I just like wearing it on my left hand." I'm thinking to myself that's kind of odd. Not married but you have a beautiful diamond ring on your ring finger of your left hand. Why is that, I thought?

Here I go, "Mouth in motion before brain is in gear." I said, "Well, you probably should wear it on your right hand, unless you're keeping it on your left to ward off people like me." She smiled and said, "I have never thought about that but since you mentioned it, might not be such a bad idea to keep in on the left hand." Well, I thought that I had crashed and burned with what she had just said. It was a very good comeback to my smartass statement, I'd have to admit.

I knew beyond a shadow of a doubt that I had NO chance with this beautiful girl. Here I was, an Ole Mississippi boy, standing in front of a woman that in my eyes was so beautiful that she would have made Lady Godiva jealous. But being the eternal optimist that I am, I threw caution into the wind and decided to introduce myself.

I said, "Hi, I'm Mike! What is your name?" She said, "My name is Mary." At that very instant I had confirmation of what I had thought the first moment that I had laid eyes on Mary: "I WAS IN LOVE"!

I never had believed in "Love, at first sight," but now I was a believer. She had the most beautiful smile and the nicest disposition. When she had said, "My name is Mary," she had extended her hand which I had not expected. I took it and the moment that we touched I knew that I was a goner. Her touch sent chills through my body like I had never encountered in my entire life! I knew that there was no doubt about it; Michael Van Buren Latch was in love!

I thanked her and said, "I'll see you tomorrow" to which she responded, "OK, I'll be here." As I was walking out the door the urge to turn and look at Mary one more time was unbearable, so that was what I did. The moment that I turned, my heart melted even more than initially. Because Mary was already looking my way and her smile was really big. But there was something else. What was it? It looked as though there was a twinkle in her eye. That was what it was exactly! Mary had a twinkle in her eye! Damn I thought! This girl might like me after all.

Chapter Three

When I got to class that morning I was a different person. All that I could concentrate on was Mary, Mary, and more Mary. I knew in my heart of hearts that it was possible that Mary and Mike would be together, forever! This beautiful angel had a hold on me like no other woman had ever had before.

I thought that I had been in love when I was in high school. Trust me, that was nothing compared to this. Back then it had taken me two or three months to tell my girlfriend at the time how I felt. I had to be coaxed into that. She was telling me that she loved me before I knew what was happening. I couldn't muster the courage to repeat that same thing to her. When she had broken up with me I thought that there was no way that I would ever love again. But within a week I was out on a date, and my former girlfriend was nothing but a memory.

With Mary though, I loved her now and we had just met. How was this possible? I had no idea and really didn't care. What I cared about was Mary. One thing that I was sure of, I would be the first to say "I love you" this time. Mary would not have to coax me as my former girlfriend did. No sir! "I loved Mary" and I could not wait until I would have the opportunity to tell her that.

Even so, I didn't offer myself much hope because of Mary's beauty. Not that I was unattractive: it was just that I had never considered myself attractive. But you never know what will happen unless you try.

I knew that there was no way Mary could feel the same as I did, I was sure! Well, I was glad that what I thought was completely wrong! I didn't know it at the time while sitting in class that morning, but Mary was thinking of me as well. Mary would later say, "The moment that you opened your mouth, I knew that you were the one and I was hooked."

Unknown to me, Mary was dating someone at the time that we met. I had no idea and wouldn't until after we had been together a few months, but I am getting ahead of myself here. All that I cared about was trying to figure out a way to make amends for acting like an idiot about the ring thing and seeing what happened from there. I had to make sure that my plan, the plan to make her want to meet me or go out with me on a date, went the way that I wanted it to go.

On my way back to the apartment after class, I was tempted to stop back by the grocery store but I did not want it to be so obvious that I was crazy about her. I was trying to be cool, while burning up inside with desire to be with this beautiful girl.

When I returned to the apartment Ronnie was there and after telling him what happened at the grocery store he said, "Are you going to ask her out?" I said, "I probably will ask her tomorrow but she probably won't go." "Why not", Pitt asked. Pitt was and still is Ronnie's nickname to me. And I told him what I'd said in our initial meeting. Pitt said, "Ask her out. There are only two things that she can say. Yes or no. So bow your neck like when we were playing baseball and let-it-rip."

I knew that Pitt was right, and I had already made up my mind that I would ask Mary out or at least ask her to meet me somewhere. Yeah, that would be better. If Mary accepted a meeting invitation then I might have a chance. The only problem was that if she rejected me then I would truly crash and burn. Hell, I had crashed and burned before and always survived. With Mary, I didn't know if I would or could survive her rejection.

I know what I'll do if she rejects my initial query, I thought. I'll try a different approach. No matter what, I would not give up until the most beautiful girl that I had ever laid eyes on finally went out with me.

There was no doubt in my mind that Mary probably thought I was an idiot by what I had said that morning concerning the ring being on her left hand instead of her right since it wasn't a wedding ring. But Hell, I might as well take a chance because as Pitt said there were only two things she can say. It was either "Yes or no." And I was damned and determined that I would not take no for an answer!

The following morning I went back to the grocery store to get some gum because I still had enough cigarettes to get me through the day. When I walked in, there she was in all of her radiant beauty smiling like she was the happiest person in the world. Little did I know that she was smiling because I had just walked in!

When she saw the gum in my hand she said, "What, no cigarettes today?" There I stood in my starched button-down Ralph Lauren Polo adjusting my trademark visor, when I said, "No, I have enough to last me today." Then without hesitation, out came the words as if someone else were saying them. I said, "Mary, if you aren't doing anything tomorrow night I will be at Abby's Irish Rose. I would love for you to come down and I would be more than happy to buy you a drink." Mary looked at me for a moment, which seemed like an eternity, before she said, "I don't know if I will be able to make it but I'll try. But I don't drink all that much."

I'm stunned initially by her response. I was also thinking that she was about to say thanks but no thanks, yet she said something that was completely different. This caught me completely off guard, but I did manage to say "Great!" Then I stood there babbling about how ladies should not be drinking all that much. All the time I was thinking, "What the hell did I just say"? Guys want girls to drink, to get tipsy, to make it easier to get them out of their clothes and have sex.

Here I was expounding on the virtues of not drinking that much to a woman that I had only known for twenty four hours. There was no doubt that I was in love. Deep, double deep, in love!

As I was heading out of the door, I turned and said, "Mary, I hope to see you there and have a great day." "You have a great day as well Mike," she said. Wow, after all the worrying about whether Mary would even consider meeting me much less going out with me, I had a chance! As I walked out the door I felt like I was walking on air, hoping and praying that she would be at Abby's that night.

Chapter Four

Well, Pitt and I had gotten to Abby's Irish Rose apparently a wee bit too early on that Wednesday night because when Mary did arrive I was about "three sheets in the wind." I could still carry on a conversation, although not too intelligently. There was no doubt now that I was a complete idiot in her eyes by being intoxicated. Probably not far from the truth, but in my defense I thought that since she had not already arrived earlier, she wasn't coming to meet me. So I began to drink Kamikazes with a vengeance.

I had been wondering why she hadn't shown up, thinking with every shot, "I don't care if she comes or not". Well I knew beyond a shadow of a doubt that I was lying to myself with that thought. I had Mary on the brain and there was NO turning back. She had been on my mind constantly! She was the only one for me even though we had only met on Monday and now this was Wednesday. Man I was "hooked"! She could have told me to do anything and I would have jumped at the opportunity.

I remembered looking at the clock. It was nine fifty, and I sat there thinking "well, not tonight," when all of a sudden there was Mary walking down the stairs. The most beautiful girl I had ever seen had arrived. With her black hair flowing, white teeth glistening, Mary descended the stairs while smiling at ME! The Ole Mississippi boy was being singled out with that beautiful smile of hers. This made my heart melt.

All of a sudden the smile began to fade. Mary had apparently realized that I was somewhat intoxicated. After she had descended the stairs and was within five feet of me Mary said, "How long have you been here Mike?" I told her about three hours, and she said, "My goodness, you're drunk."

I immediately tried to defend myself by saying that I didn't think that she was coming so I decided to drown my sorrows. Mary would have none of that. Mary said, "Well I think that it would be best if someone drove you home. You are in no position to drive." My reply was, "Who do you have in mind?" She said, "Get Ronnie to drive you home." I told her that Pitt and I had arrived in separate vehicles. Pitt was supposed to go see Betty Jean, Pitt's girlfriend, later on that night. Mary asked me if there was anyone else that I could call and even though there were a few, I said, "Nope, I guess if you don't want me to drive then you will have to drive me home."

I was thinking that, since Mary seemed somewhat pissed at me, that this would probably be the one and only time we would be alone together. So I needed to make the most of the time that I was about to have. Not that it would be all that long, since the drive from the Rose to the apartment complex where I lived would take approximately five minutes. That was, if Mary decided to drive me at all. Mary thought about it for a moment and then said, "Ok. I'll drive you home" and we headed out the door.

I'm thinking on the way to her car well, she may be pissed but she likes me or she wouldn't be driving me home. Or was that wishful thinking? When I reached to kiss her after we had approached her car I realized that it was wishful thinking because she avoided my approach. Mary not letting me kiss her made me like her, want her, and adore her even more.

Mary was not going to be easy catch. I had my work cut out for me that was for sure. Looking back I am glad that she wasn't easy. Several girls at Ole Miss had been "easy," if you know what I mean. My Mary was NOT one of them!

When we arrived at the apartment complex I asked her to take me to Leon's and Billy's, two friends of mine from Booneville, Mississippi. I had met them both in some of my classes. Leon was a huge 76'er fan along with Dr. J and I was a huge Celtic fan with "The Hick from French Lick, Larry Bird." I would go over to their apartment, usually on Sunday afternoon, and we would watch the NBA, especially if the Sixers were playing my beloved Celtics.

So that particular night I wanted to see what Leon and Billy were doing. I asked Mary to take me there. I did not really want to go home at such an early hour, ten thirty, so why not go to Leon's and Billy's. Maybe they would have some more alcohol. Being somewhat inebriated, that was what I thought that I needed at that moment. Boy was I wrong with that thought! Plus what college senior goes to bed at ten thirty? This one wasn't going to, that was for sure. The following morning I regretted the decision I made that night immensely.

We got to Leon's and Billy's; Mary said that she wanted to make sure that I got up the stairs OK. So she walked the stairs with me to Leon's and Billy's door. I knocked on the door and when Leon answered, I thought the proper thing to do was to introduce them. I don't remember exactly what I said and based on what Leon said I mumbled, it went something like this: "Leon this is Mary, Mary this is Leon. Leon don't you think she is the most beautiful girl in the world?" To which Leon would tell me the following morning that my speech was slurred to say the least, but that he did think that Mary was beautiful!

Apparently, what I thought I said and what I actually said were two different things. Here is what Leon told me I said: Mary stated that she was leaving and I started begging her not to go. All the while as she was walking down the stairs to her car I kept yelling, "NO, please don't leave Mary. If you leave then I will jump!" Leon said that I climbed up on the railing acting as if I was planning to jump. I thought that if I hurt myself Mary wouldn't leave.

Leon said I repeated myself again, "Mary if you leave I will jump." And she responded, "Go ahead fool and jump because I'm leaving." Leon told me that he and Billy burst out laughing at what Mary said. They helped me down from the railing because they thought that I might actually fall accidentally, hurting myself as Mary drove away.

Leon, along with Billy's assistance, helped me inside their apartment. I proceeded to lie down on their living room floor and pass out. The next morning Leon told me all that happened, word for word or as he said, "This is the best that I could understand with the way you were slurring your words." Well, I just continue to make an ass of myself, I told Leon. I knew for certain that Mary was done with me for good now.

I was hoping that the twinkle I had seen in her eye on Tuesday morning had been real and not a figment of my imagination. If it was real, then maybe, just maybe, I would get a second chance. Hopefully Mary was thinking that she could and would 'tame' the Ole Mississippi boy!

There was no doubt that I had blown the first date, even though it was actually a meeting, with Mary. I had let myself be a victim of alcohol. Now I had ruined my only shot, to be with the most beautiful girl that I had ever seen.

Chapter Five

After clearing the cobwebs from the hangover and shaving and showering, I sat in the apartment and thought to myself: "I am not going to let this woman get away from me. Yes, I was stupid last night, but that is beside the point. I know in my heart that I Love Mary. I am not giving up that easy. If I have to eat crow then that is what I will do. I will not go down without a fight!"

I thought about what I would say when I walked into the Sunflower grocery store again. Would I pretend that nothing had happened? No, I couldn't do that because it would make me look foolish. Plus it might say to Mary that I didn't care about her. There would have been absolutely no truth in that whatsoever! I was nuts about the angel. No doubt about it at all.

I wanted as well as needed to be honest. If I wasn't honest with Mary in the beginning then we would have absolutely nothing to build our relationship on. That was the way I had been raised, and if I could not be honest with Mary in the beginning then we had no chance for a future. If she rejected my apology initially then I would try something else. Send her flowers! Send her a card! Anything that would get her to forgive me for the way I had acted. I needed, wanted, and had to have a second chance because Mary was the one for me!

I contemplated this for a long time and decided that when I saw Mary again I would apologize from the bottom of my heart. I would tell her that what happened that night at Abby's Irish Rose was not me at all. I would tell her that I was sorry for embarrassing her, for making an ass out of myself in front of people that she had just met, and plead for another chance. I wanted a chance to show her that I was a good person, not the idiot that she had witnessed Wednesday night.

That was my plan. Now I was ready to walk into the Sunflower and face the music as they say. I would grovel, beg, plead, you name it, and I was ready to do it! Every part of my being wanted a second chance and there was nothing that I wouldn't do for one more opportunity to be with Mary.

As I walked into the grocery store on that Thursday morning, I noticed instantly and to my amazement that Mary was not at her usual register. She wasn't anywhere! She was probably on a break or doing something else was the first thing that entered my simple and hung-over brain. Then after about five minutes of wandering around the store and waiting for Mary to appear, I became concerned. She was nowhere to be seen. I kinda freaked for moment thinking, "Did she get home Ok?" I had no idea how far she had to drive after she had delivered my drunken ass to Leon's and Billy's. Now my mind is racing ninety to nothing trying to imagine every possible reason for Mary not being there.

Since I did not have her number or know where she lived I would have to wait until the following day to find out the answer to the racing questions in my head. I was about to leave when I saw this oriental gentleman with a Sunflower apron on. I said, "Sir, excuse me please, but could you tell me at what time the young lady that is normally here will be working again?" He said, "She will be back tomorrow. Today is her day off." Whew I thought! Thank goodness she is Ok, I thought, because Riki, (that was what was on his name tag) had just said that she would be there tomorrow. I thanked him and headed out the door.

On the way out it struck me that something still could have happened to Mary. The gentleman that I had just spoken with would not have known that something might be wrong until she did not show up for work the following morning. Then he would be concerned and then it might be too late to save her! I would not have worried, had I known who Riki was at the time, but I didn't.

When I got back to the apartment, it was time to drown my sorrows. The only problem with that was I was so hung over that getting that first beer down was all that I could do. One beer was too much and I poured most of it out. Man had I been an idiot the night before. That beer tasted worse than anything that I had ever put in my mouth. No more alcohol for awhile. Maybe never drinking again crossed my mind for a moment. What had it done for me anyway? Alcohol did nothing but make me act like a damn idiot along with possibly ruining the only chance that I would have with the most beautiful girl that I had ever seen. It was time to hit the books to study for an upcoming test. But who was I kidding? I was concerned about Mary!

I began thinking, Oh man; don't let anything bad have happened to Mary! I had been thinking this the remainder of that day as well as the afternoon and now it was night and I was still thinking the same thing. Finally, I fell asleep. It seemed that I tossed and turned all night and I could not wait for daybreak to come to get to the Sunflower to see if "My Mary" was OK. She didn't know that she was mine at that time, but I did!

I had made a complete ass of myself in front of the woman that I wanted to be with and now I would have to wait another day to make sure that she was Ok. I prayed to God that she was and then I could apologize for my stupid and childish behavior

When I awoke that following morning the first thing that popped in my brain was "I was praying to God that Mary is alright. If she is alright and she doesn't forgive me then that is Ok. As long as she is fine is all that I want at this very moment." Yes, I wanted Mary, but her safety meant more to me than anything else right then.

In my heart I needed Mary's forgiveness and I needed that second chance. I had no idea what Mary was thinking. Did she hate me? Did she think that I was just a dumb Ole Mississippi boy who didn't know how to act around a lady? Wondering what she was thinking was tearing me up inside. Later Mary would tell me that she had thought that I was an ass and she hadn't decided whether I deserved a second chance or not when I walked in that Thursday morning.

Mary was dating someone else when I had met her but all she could think about was the way I sounded when I spoke as she would tell me later in our relationship. American by Birth and Southern by the Grace of God would be what I would tell her several months down the road. But again I am getting ahead of myself.

All I can say is, "Thank God for the Southern Accent!" She was hooked just as much as I was and I didn't even know it. Wish that I had though, since it would have made my life a lot easier and a lot less worrisome. I had to work for this relationship and it made it much more meaningful.

Chapter Six

Friday morning came and not soon enough. I jumped out of bed, went into the bathroom to shave, brush my teeth and take a shower. I wanted to present myself in the best possible way in hopes that Mary would like what she saw, accept my apology, and maybe, just maybe, go out with me on a "real date."

I normally don't take very long to get ready because usually I don't care what people think about the way I look. Now was a totally different story. If I didn't know better myself, I would have thought that I was getting ready for a book signing or a trip to the Oscars.

It took me so long that I knew that I would have to miss my first class if I wanted to see Mary and apologize to her. At that instant in my life there was nothing else that mattered more than my apology to Mary. A genie could have appeared and said, "I'll give you anything you want. A contract with any team in the Major League; a job making a ton of money; anything you want and all you have to do is take it this very moment." My reply would have been, "Sorry, you will have to wait until I see the Love of my Life or it is a no go." I am serious when I say that Mary had a hold on me like no other woman ever had before.

I was in love, enthralled, smitten, head-over-heels, you name it, and that was the way you could describe how I felt about Mary. Now all I had to do was to convince her that she should give me a second chance. I had to be on my best behavior and sweep her off of her feet and live happily ever after. This would be a piece of cake, right? I was hoping beyond hope, but no matter what, I would not give up, no way!

When I left the apartment all that I could think about was "Is she at work?" "Is she Ok?" "Will she forgive me?" "Will she think I am an idiot?" Well, I had acted like an idiot that fateful night at Abby's Irish Rose, so why wouldn't she? Mary had every right to not give me another opportunity. If I had been in her shoes I do not know if I would have been inclined to give me another shot, especially the way I had acted.

I am not a person that backs down from anything; well, I did at one time, although that is for a later chapter. But believe me when I say that walking into the Sunflower grocery store that morning, I was scared. I was scared first and foremost that she would not be there because something had happened on her way home the night she drove me to Leon's and Billy's. Second, that if she was there, she would be cordial and nice but not be willing to afford me a second chance. Scared, hell: I was terrified. I had met the woman for me and now because of my stupidity I lost her even before I had her.

As I entered, there she was, so I had to assume that she had made it home all right the night in question. I hate to assume anything but I was sure that she would let me know if anything had happened to her once she had dropped me off. At least I thought that she would, but then again who am I kidding. I had only known of this woman's existence since Monday of this week and now it was Friday. Why would she confide in me if something had happened? She wouldn't give me the time of day was what I concluded, so why should I even go in to apologize? Just make a fool of myself again? No! I wanted as well as needed to make a point that I am a good person and to plead my case for a second chance.

Mary had just finished with a customer and another one was standing in line as I walked into the store. Mary was being her normal self because she was conversing with the customer like they were the best of friends. Thinking that I would go unnoticed because of the conversation that

Mary was having, I eased by real quick to go undetected. Whew, she didn't see me, I thought. Now I can approach at my leisure.

That morning at my apartment I had stood in front of the mirror trying to rehearse the right things that would make Mary want to give me a second chance. Each time that I had reviewed or gone over my speech, I fouled it up unmercifully. Now here I was in the Sunflower starting to perspire. Damn, what was wrong with the deodorant? Did I forget to put it on? That couldn't be the problem because that was one thing that I never forgot. I detested smelly people, so not putting on deodorant was not the issue. The issue here was I was afraid that Mary would not give me the second chance that I desperately wanted and needed. Mary seemed to be in a good mood. Maybe I would get that second chance.

I contemplated not apologizing but there was no way out without being seen. If Mary noticed me leaving without saying hello much less apologizing then it would definitely be over for sure. Damn it I thought! I was stuck now!

I decided that my need, along with the desire, to apologize outweighed the fear that I had about what Mary might actually say when I approached her. Mary was nice enough to care for me on Wednesday night so the least I could do would be to say I was sorry for the way I acted that night and then leave.

Once Mary had finished with the lady I waited maybe an additional minute or two and then headed to the cash register. I'm thinking that she had no idea that I am even in the store. The moment I walked up Mary said, "I saw you come in. What took you so long?" I am embarrassed, and astonished that she noticed me coming in when she was as busy as she had been upon my entry.

Instead of trying to come up with an excuse as to why I had been waiting, I told her this: "Mary, I came by yesterday to apologize and you weren't here. I was afraid that something had happened to you until the little oriental man said that you would be here today. Then I thought, well he hoped, that you would be here today but he had no idea for sure since you as well as he were employees of Sunflower."

At that moment Mary started laughing and I asked her what was so funny, to which she replied, "That little oriental man is Japanese and he is my 'Daddy'." I am sure that I had a look of surprise was on my face and I remember saying "really" and Mary said, "Yes really. That is my Daddy, Riki." I said that I had noticed his name tag yesterday and thought that Riki was spelled in an odd way, but who am I to judge how someone spells their name.

I then asked Mary what her last name was and when she pronounced it, a light went off in my head. Mary went on to say that she was Japanese/American and then I understood, because Mary did look somewhat like Riki's culture but not so much that I could connect the dots. Now I knew why Riki was sure that Mary would be at work today. I had come to find out Riki "owned" the Sunflower grocery store, so he was the "boss man" as Mary would call him!

Well, now thanks to Mary, the proverbial ice had been broken somewhat and was broken even more when Mary said, "Is there something that you wanted to say to me, Mike?" I told Mary the following: "I had everything that I wanted to say on the tip of my tongue and now I can't remember exactly how it was supposed to go." Mary said, "Well why don't you try letting it flow from your heart. If you really mean it then it should not be all that difficult."

And this is what I said to the best of my recollection: "Mary, I want to apologize from the bottom of my heart for the way I acted Wednesday night. In no way was that the real me. Normally I am not a drunk, but that night I was and there are no excuses for my behavior. What I would like to ask is for your forgiveness. I promise that if you will give me a second chance, then what happened Wednesday night will never happen again!"

I stood there for what seemed like an eternity as Mary thought about what I had just said. She was kinda looking through me in a way and then I noticed a twinkle in her eye, like the twinkle that I had seen on that Monday that we had first met. By looking into her eyes I knew instantly that I would get my second chance before the words ever came out of her mouth.

Mary said, "Mike, I don't like people who are unruly, rude, abrasive, and abusive and anything else that makes me feel uncomfortable and especially people who drink too much." Boy I must have misread that twinkle was what I was thinking when I heard the remainder of her words. Which were, "The other night you were unruly and you had way too much to drink, don't you think?" Whew, this is bad so I must be really misreading the twinkles. At least she didn't say that I was rude, abusive or abrasive. But Mary had said enough, and I was about to say it was nice meeting you when she said something else that took me by surprise. Mary said, "But Mike, there is something about you that I like, so what did you have in mind?"

I had hoped that she would give me a second chance, but I was stunned as well! Knowing me, even though I am never at a loss for words, it probably took me a few seconds to say, "Would you like to go out with me on a real date sometime?" When she said that sounded nice and she would like to do that, I felt like I was dreaming again! I think I may have actually pinched myself to make sure that this wasn't a dream. This was better than I could have ever had hoped for. Here was the most beautiful girl I had ever seen giving this Ole Mississippi Boy a second chance.

I proceeded to ask Mary for her number and her address and then asked when it would be convenient for me to call her and talk on the phone to discuss when and where we would go. Mary replied, "Why don't you call me tonight?" I then asked what time would be good for her because I wanted to make sure that I didn't screw this up the second time around. Mary said, "Around six or seven will be fine. We should be finished with dinner by then." I told her OK, I will call you around six or seven. I knew all along it would be closer to six than seven because I wanted to talk to this angel as soon as possible.

I said as I was about to leave, "Thanks Mary for the second chance. You won't regret it" to which she replied, "Don't screw it up this time Mike because there won't be another." My response was "Don't worry, I won't."

On my way to class after leaving the Sunflower grocery all that I could think about was talking to Mary that night. It seemed like I was back in high school and not in college the way I felt. Isn't it strange how you feel when you are in love? A strange but yet a very satisfying and all consuming feeling that makes you get weak in the knees.

Chapter Seven

That day in class time flew by. I mean it was like I had just sat down and it was time to get up and go to the next one. Normally it is the other way around when there is something that you want to do so badly you can "taste" it, but this was not the case this time. I was thinking "this is too good to be true. Surely something will happen that will prevent us from going out." I consider myself an eternal optimist, and yet I was taking a pessimistic approach.

When I got back to the apartment Pitt was there and he asked if I had stopped by the grocery store to apologize and what had happened. I told him what unfolded and he said, "Awesome!" I had a few hours to kill so I started studying and the more that I tried concentrating on Micro-Economics the less I retained. All I could think about was where to take Mary on our first date. One place I knew damn well we were not going was Abby's Irish Rose. But where and then it dawned on me, The Beacon! They had everything that you could imagine, so I was sure that we could find something there that we would both like.

Six o'clock rolled around that Friday night and it was within the time frame that Mary had given me so I grabbed the phone and called. A lady, who I found out later on, was Mary's mom, Reba, answered the phone. I said in the most polite way, "May I speak to Mary please?" Mary's mom asked who was calling and I told her it was Mike, a friend of Mary's. Mary's mom told me to wait for a moment and soon Mary was on the other end.

You see, remember I mentioned earlier that Mary was dating someone else. Mary and this other guy had only been dating for about two or three months and now I was in the picture. Or at least I was hoping that I was in the picture and actually the "main attraction" in Mary's eyes.

Mary's mom really liked the other guy and now here I was calling to speak to her daughter. This did not go over very well, with Mary's mom. I had upset the proverbial apple cart by intruding into Mary's life, or that was what I thought. I knew or should I say that I hoped Mary's parents would let her make her own decisions about who she went out with. Which, thank God they did.

When Mary got on the phone I immediately asked how the remainder of her day had gone. She said that it had been busy but not that bad. Her dad had let her off early. I wanted to know all about Mary but I also wanted to save some for our dinner conversation. Mary proceeded to tell me that she had not been in Oxford all that long. Her family had moved back because her mother's mom was ill. Mary's mother's mother lived in Ecru, Mississippi, which was not all that far from Oxford. Mary told me that her dad had owned grocery stores in the greater Los Angeles area, so it was only natural for him to open one when he came to Oxford.

Mary talked about growing up in Los Angeles, California. I inquired as to how many brothers and sisters she had, and Mary said that she had one brother, Richard, living with her and her parents along with Cindy her middle sister. Mary said that her older sister Pam was still in California. That was it, other than all of the felines that they had. Mary asked about me and I said that I was an only child, to which she said immediately, "I bet you're spoiled." I said that I had been for quite some time but had grown out of it over the years.

We continued to talk about various things and then I popped the question. "Mary, would you like to go to dinner tomorrow night?" I knew that this was really quick but I thought the sooner that we got together for a date the better.

She responded with a yes and I thought that I was about to float off of the bed. I told her that she could pick anywhere her heart desired and she said that she had rather I do that. I told her that I thought The Beacon would be a good place if that was alright with her. Mary agreed, so the place was set. Now all I needed for our date to go off without any problems, Mary to have a "fantastic" time, and maybe I would get the girl of my dreams. Mary said, "Would seven o'clock be Ok with you?" Even though I wanted to pick her up at four that Saturday afternoon, I said that would be fine with me.

I now had a real date scheduled with the most beautiful girl I had ever seen and I was going to make damn sure that I didn't screw this up!

Chapter Eight

I t seemed like it took forever for Saturday morning and afternoon to go by. Each time that I looked at the clock it was like time was standing still. I decided that I needed to get the car washed and cleaned up since I didn't want to make a bad impression with a dirty car.

All that I could concentrate on was Mary and our date. I was so head over heels in love I didn't know what to do. Cleaning the car helped, though, and after that was over it was time to go to the cleaners and get the dry cleaning that had been there for a week. Yeah, I had forgotten about it with Mary on the brain, but that was OK. The remainder of Saturday afternoon was spent watching sports on the tube and wishing that time would fly by.

By four that Saturday afternoon, I started to count the hours like a child would do on Christmas Eve. I had no idea what I would happen that night. I knew what I wanted to happen. I wanted Mary to have the "best time that she had ever had." After that all I wanted was a good night kiss. No hanky panky, just a kiss. Now don't misunderstand the no hanky panky, because I was definitely interested but I really, really, really, really, really liked this girl so I was going to be on my best behavior.

When I got dressed that night with my Levi's, buttoned down Ralph Lauren Polo, and Nike's, I decided to add little fragrance. I selected Polo cologne by Ralph Lauren. Great decision on my part because the moment that Mary opened the door and she said "You smell nice Mike." Although my given name is Michael, everyone called me Mike. Mary could have called me anything that she had wanted to and I would have answered. I told her thanks and then commented that she smelled very nice as well.

Nice, hell it was Intoxicating. Here I am about to go on a date with the most beautiful, best smelling woman I had ever been with. Couldn't get any better than this, or so I thought!

We went to dinner at The Beacon and we started to talk, and suddenly it dawned on me that this is the woman that I had been looking for all my life. Now all I had to do was to hold on to her and my life would be complete.

Mary talked about, Richard and her sisters, Cindy and Pam. She talked about what they were doing. Cindy was into aerobics and Richard was into Dungeons and Dragons and Pam was working in California. When it came time to talk about me, there was not that much to talk about with the exception of my parents and my best friend Pitt. No brothers or sisters, but I did have a little short haired peek-a-poo name Peanut. We talked about Mary growing up in the big city of Los Angeles and me in rural Mississippi. City girl with a country boy! How do you like them potatoes?

We talked about everything it seemed and when dinner was finished, I felt as if I had known Mary all my life. Wow, what a feeling! The connection that we had was surreal and mind boggling. I was feeling like the luckiest man in the world and this was only the first date. I had to hold on to this woman: there were no ifs, ands, or buts about it. Mary was going to be mine and mine forever.

After dinner I decided that I wanted to make a really good impression on her as well as her parents, so I thought it would be a smart move to get her home at a reasonable hour. While driving back to Mary's parents' home all that I could think about was if she would kiss me if I made a move. You know, not one of those pecks on the cheek or a quick one on the lips, but a "real kiss."

When we pulled in the drive I told Mary that I had a fantastic time and she replied, "I did as well Mike." While thinking about the kiss I was also, being able to multi-task, thinking about when to ask her out again. As we were getting out of the car I said, "Mary, since you and I both had a really nice time tonight, why don't we do this again real soon." Mary replied, "I think that would be nice. Why don't you call me tomorrow?" Wow, I was in "High Cotton now"! That is a Mississippi saying when things are really going well. And to me they were not just going well. They were *FANTASTIC*!

Now as I walked Mary to her front door I was still apprehensive about the kiss, but I thought "What the Hell" and went for it! Man, oh man, was I glad that I took the chance. Damn right I was! We kissed and kissed and kissed. Not just me kissing Mary, but Mary was kissing me back. You could feel the passion in the kiss and it was starting to have a certain effect on me, if you know what I mean.

When we were finished kissing and I was about to leave I told Mary how great of a time that I had, again. As I was about to turn and go to my car I reached for her again and we enjoyed another spine tingling kiss. Damn I love kissing this girl, and I wanted to make it a regular occurrence.

That was the beginning of a relationship that would take us into 1981 and should have taken us farther. But I will get to that later.

Chapter Nine

For the next two years or so Mary and I were inseparable. We used to ride around in her dad's rag top VW drinking a bottle of bubbly every now and then. We would drive out to Sardis, sit and, talk about our future. We made plans and as far as I was concerned, there was nothing in the world that would alter the plans we were making.

We went to Ole Miss Football games and to several concerts. I even gave Mary her first pair of diamond earrings, and she looked beautiful wearing them. Cindy would later tell her that she was somewhat jealous and had dropped one down the drain in the sink in the bathroom by accident. Cindy said that she had to take the pipe drain apart. Lucky for her the earring was in the elbow of the pipe. Mary rarely gets mad or upset, but I am sure that would have "lit a fire" in her, had Cindy not been able to get the earring out.

One concert in particular stands out in my mind because that was the first time that Mary and I became intimate with one another. Mary, Pitt, Betty Jean, who was Pitt's main squeeze at the time, and I were attending a Willie Nelson concert. On the way into the concert we were told that the UPD, University Police Department, was checking purses for concealed contraband, aka whiskey. Pitt took Betty's and Mary's purses and sat them beside a window of the Coliseum before we went inside. Once we were through security and in the Coliseum, Pitt ran over to the window, reached out and retrieved them. We thought that we were so cool because we had outsmarted the UPD, and we were. You had to have a bottle of Jack Daniel's at a Willie Nelson Concert. Now we had two and it was party time at Ole Miss! I was in heaven: The most beautiful girl on the Ole Miss Campus with me at a Willie Nelson concert and a bottle of Jack Daniel's. What else could I want that night?

I knew that I wanted to be intimate with Mary that night, but I thought that there was no chance of that happening. As the night continued I hoped that Mary wanted me as well. I was sure that she didn't but later I found out that I had been wrong.

I remember all of us along with Ricky and his date down on the floor and Willie coming out right to the edge of the stage. Ricky yelled up to Willie and in an instant tossed the bottle toward Willie. He grabbed the bottle out of the air, took the top off, took a big swig, put the top back on, dropped it back to Ricky and said, "Thank you Son." Then he began singing, "On the Road Again" and we went nuts! Willie Nelson had partaken of our Jack and now he was singing his latest hit.

I thought that we would go there to be alone and really had no idea that we would be intimate that night. Once we were there and it was determined that Pitt and Betty would not be there any time in the near future, we proceeded to become passionate with one another. One thing led to another and the night turned into total bliss for both of us. The intimacy with Mary was very special to me, because Mary loved me and her passion said that she was in love me as well. I knew then and there that I wanted to spend the rest of my life with Mary! Not to go into great detail but it needs to be said that the event that night was the most special thing that had happened to me in all of my adult years because I made love to the woman that I was in love with.

I would say to Mary later after we had been dating for awhile, "Mary, it was my 'bubbly personality' that got me the second chance, wasn't it?" To which she replied, "Ha Ha. It might have been but the main thing was your voice. I cannot explain how it makes me feel. There is just something about the way you sounded and I loved it. I think that the moment that I saw you, and you opened your mouth, that I was just as hooked as you were."

Once I graduated from Ole Miss, Mary and I stayed very close with one another. I was working for Hankins Lumber Company out of Grenada, Mississippi, so it was easy to see her within two hours. It actually tore me apart when Mary, along with her mother, dad, sister, and brother went to California to visit Pam, Mary's older sister. I had been with Mary nearly every waking moment and now she was gone. All I could do was talk to her on the phone, which we did as much as possible. I do not remember how long she was actually gone, but I can tell you that it seemed like it was forever.

When I found out that Mary would be coming home, I was a kid again on Christmas Eve. I could not wait for the day for her and her family to arrive back in Oxford. It made no difference to me where I was supposed to be, because the only thing that mattered was seeing "My Mary."

I was in my hometown of Corinth when I got the news and I immediately planned on being in Oxford the day after she arrived. You might wonder why the day after and not the same day? It was difficult for me to wait, but I knew that she would probably be tired from the trip back. I wanted to make sure that she was rested before I came bouncing in. While they were in California I even stayed at Mary's parents and took care of the felines. That's right! I must have been in love, because here you had an avid dog person taking care of a bunch of cats. Love does strange things to a man, and it certainly did to me.

In the fall of 1980 I was offered a position in Memphis with an industrial supply company. Once I had made the decision to take the job and move there, I thought that the only thing that was missing in my life was Mary. I wanted her with me on a full time basis. I had only one thing on my mind: Mary. To be complete I wanted to marry her, have a family with her, and live happily ever after. Nothing else mattered but Mary and being happy with Mary forever!

I remember going to Oxford one weekend to visit Mary. My decision had been made before I had left Memphis for Oxford that I would ask Mary to come to Memphis to live with me. While we were out on a date one Saturday night, having a great time as usual, I decided to ask her a very important question: I said, "Mary I would really like, no love for you to move in with me in Memphis. That way we can be together all the time and we can start to plan our lives together." I had no idea the response that I would get, but the one I got was definitely the one that I had hoped for. Mary said, "Is that what you really want Mike, because if it is, that is what I want as well." I had to ask again because I was sure that my hearing had just "tanked" and when Mary said, "Yes, Mike I would love to move in and live with you," I was in "High Cotton" all over again. I told Mary that she had just made me the happiest person in world, and we started discussing when she would arrive.

Chapter Ten

Everything had been great with Mary and me since she had moved in. I was working, she was taking care of the apartment, cooking, doing laundry, and we were two people "in love." I could not wait to get home at night to see my darling Mary, the woman that was going to be my wife. All I had to do was ask Mary to marry me, for her say yes, and we would get married and live happily ever after.

One instance stands out more than any other. Mary called me at work one day asking if I would like to come home for lunch and have a home cooked meal. Who was she kidding with that request? She knew that I would jump at that opportunity to have lunch with my darling Mary.

At high noon I headed out the door to go home and have a wonderful cooked meal with my darling Mary. Mary was a fabulous cook, in that she was willing to try and try until she got it right. More times than not she would succeed in cooking the meal to perfection, even though she might have to try it two or three times.

The only thing that I remember Mary being disgusted with was a peach cobbler pie that my mother cooked that would melt in your mouth. Mary tried this no fewer than ten times, and she could never get it correct. She even went as far as to say one time, "I think that you mother has left something out of the recipe and she wants me to fail." Mary knew that was not true because my mother as well as my dad adored her. She was just frustrated that she couldn't make the peach cobbler the way that my mom did. I guess there are some things that only mothers can do!

When I arrived at our apartment I knocked on the door because even though I had a key I had asked Mary to lock both deadbolts when I left that morning. Even though we lived in a safe neighborhood, you never know, anything could happen even when you are as prepared as you can be. I would have died if anything had happened to my Mary, so I did not want her to take any chances at all.

The response from the other side of the door was, "Who is it please?", like she was expecting someone else. I said, "It's me, darling, Mike." I heard the locks being unlocked and ever so slowly the door begins to open. I'm standing there wondering why it is taking so long for Mary to open the door. I am also wondering what was going on since she normally opened the door immediately and was standing there to greet me when I came home at night, with a hug and a kiss.

When the door finally opened there was no Mary in front of me but then I heard her say, "Why don't you come on in mister", which I did immediately. Let's just say that when I saw Mary standing behind the door that was one of the best, if not the best surprises that I have ever had in my life. Seeing Mary there in her birthday suit, I knew immediately that lunch would have to wait! But I didn't care one bit at all.

Mary was everyman's dream, and I had to pinch myself sometimes to realize that she actually was living with me, loving me, and that we were planning our future together. There was not a day that went by that we failed to tell one another how much we loved being together, how much we loved one another, and how much we were in love with one another. We would do anything for each other and there is no finer example than what happened in October of 1980.

In fall of 1980, the apartment complex where we were living was having a costume contest for Halloween. Mary wanted us to dress up as Mickey and Minnie Mouse. I didn't really want to do this because I thought that it was a bit "cheesy," no pun intended. But since she had gone to all of the trouble to get the mouse ears, the white shirts, and the black pants for me along with everything thing else that was needed to make us look like Mickey and Minnie, I thought, "Ok" I can embarrass myself for the woman I love.

When we walked into the recreation area where the event was taking place we immediately received responses of "those are great costumes." I remember one person saying, "If you guys don't win then something is wrong". Well we won and Mary was beaming! That made me feel fantastic and less of a fool because of all of the hard work she had put into getting us ready. We even went to dinner after the costume party, and we went as Mickey and Minnie Mouse. I remember the waitress referring to us as that. We had a great time and it was all Mary's idea, plus all of Mary's hard work.

Chapter Eleven

Mary and I continued to do fun things after that Halloween Party in 1980. We would go to different events in the Memphis area. I think that this California girl was trying to smooth the rough edges of this Ole Mississippi boy.

I remember even going to a play one time. On the way, all I am thinking is, "what the HELL am I doing going to a sissy play." When we got there Mary's mom, Reba, dad, Riki, and sister Cindy were there. I am sure that Mary told me that they were coming but I was probably too concerned about me not enjoying the play to have remembered that they were meeting us there.

When we were seated Mary took may hand and said, "Thank you for coming. I know this is something that you probably did not want to do, but I really appreciate it very much and I hope that you enjoy it." I told her that she was welcome, and I sat back to be miserable. Enjoy a play? You have got to be kidding me, I thought. I had rather watch grass grow that to sit here and be bored out of my mind. So the play began and in only a few minutes I was totally enthralled. I can't remember now what it was about but I do remember thinking, "Damn this is alright."

Well, Mary had been correct again! I did enjoy the play and when it was over I made sure to tell that. She smiled and said, "I hoped you would and I am glad you did." Wow! This woman was special, and I was definitely going to make sure that she would be mine forever.

We continued to do all sort of things together. We would drive to Ecru, Mississippi, to visit Mary's grandmother; we would go visit my parents in Corinth, Mississippi, without me having to convince her that we should, because she was the one suggesting that we go. "Two peas in a pod" was what we were, and I was the happiest man in the world. I had the best and most beautiful girl in the world. We were going be together forever!

Chapter Twelve

I t is weird how things change almost without you sometimes realizing that it has happened. Then before you can do anything about it, it is too late.

Well, I don't really know where to begin with this or really how we got to where we ended up. What I do know is that the love of my life left me, when I thought that everything was Ok. Mary didn't leave me because she was mad or anything like that, I don't think. We never had a cross word, we got along as well or better than any two people could have ever hoped.

The beginning of the end started on a Sunday afternoon after Mary had returned from visiting her parents in Oxford. I had done the same, returning from Corinth that afternoon as well. We were sitting on the sofa talking about our visits when out of nowhere Mary said, "I think that I want to go back to college and get my degree." I was somewhat surprised by her statement but wanting to be supportive said, "That sounds great."

I thought that since we were living together, that she would go to Memphis State and finish her degree. After all, we had been discussing getting married. On several occasions we had tossed around names for the children that we planned on having once we were married. But Mary wanted to return to Ole Miss to get her degree, and I didn't think that was all that odd. I had gone there and it wasn't like she would be in another part of the country. Hell, she wouldn't be more than an hour and a half away.

Well, Mary moved out and back in with her parents. We both decided that we would still be true only each other and no one else. We had every intention of getting married; only now we would wait until Mary graduated.

I made several trips to Oxford to see Mary once she was settled back in at her parent's house. Each time that I visited, which was almost every weekend and even sometimes during the week, we would always have a great time together. It was kind of like when I was at Ole Miss and we were dating. We would on occasions have dinner at her mom and dad's, then go out on our date.

There was one time that Mary wanted me to come to Oxford for a visit and it was on a Wednesday. The reason that I remember that it was a Wednesday was I am thinking that all we had to do was wait two more days and I would be there for the weekend. Even though it was only two more days I wanted to see Mary as well. The drive to Oxford in those days was not all that easy in that it was a two lane road for the majority of the drive. Now it takes about forty five to fifty five minutes depending on the speed you are driving, when back in 1981 it could take up to an hour and a half.

The day at work had been hell! It was time for inventory and anyone who has ever done inventory for an industrial supply company knows that it takes many, many hours to get it completed. I was tired and called Mary to say that I wouldn't be coming that afternoon. I could tell in her voice that she was hurt. I decided that the best thing for me to do was to go ahead and make the trip. When Mary heard that I would be there as soon as I could she seemed to get giddy with joy.

When I got to Mary's parents house she was beaming when she opened the door. We had not seen one another in a week, but it seemed like forever the way we greeted one another. I asked Mary why she wanted me there before the weekend. Her response was simple yet meaningful when she said, "Because I love you Mike." Smiling I told her that I loved her and then asked what she had in mind for the evening.

Mary said, "Let's go visit Bobby." I thought that was strange since I had driven all the way to Oxford on a two lane road after a hell-of-a day to see her. Now, Mary wanted to go visit Bobby. I looked at her strangely I'm sure and said, "Why do you want to go see Bobby?" To which she replied, "Because he's not at home." Oh, now I knew what she meant by that! We jumped in my Datsun 280Z and headed to Bobby's.

When we arrived at Bobby's apartment I was wondering how we would get since he was not at home. Before I could say anything, Mary produced a key and opened the door.

Once inside, the intimacy that we had with one another was beyond words. There was no doubt that Mary would be my wife. I knew in my heart that we would be together forever. Boy was I wrong with that assumption. That night, was the last time that I saw Mary for the better part of a year.

When I left that Wednesday night going back to Memphis, I kissed Mary for the last time. I was supposed to go to Oxford in two days for the weekend but something came up at work and I had to work that weekend. Since I had planned on going to Corinth the next weekend to see my grandmother who was ninety two at the time, we decided that I would be back in Oxford in two weeks from the upcoming Friday.

It had been a ritual since Mary had moved back in with her parents that we would talk every night to tell each other how much we missed and loved one another. Every night turned into every other night and then it went to every third night. This happened because of the economics of the situation, not because we were drawing apart. Long distance phone calls could get expensive back then. There were no cell phones, just Maw Bell, and we both agreed that it would be best to not talk as often. We knew that we loved each other and that I could save the money to do other things with Mary. Plus, as they say, "absence makes the heart grow fonder."

So I was Ok with not talking to Mary every night or every other night, because I knew that she was "mine." Mary would be with me forever, or at least that was what I thought.

On the second week that we were supposed to talk on our new phone schedule, I called and Mary's mother Reba answered the phone. When I asked to speak to Mary I was told, "She is not here right now."

I politely asked Reba to tell Mary that I had called. Reba said that she would so I expected Mary to call me upon her return.

Well, there was no call that night, so I tried again the following night, and I was told the same exact thing as the previous night: "I am sorry, Mary is not here." Over the next week I called every day to speak to Mary and was told by her mother that she wasn't there. I would leave a message with her mother, asking her to let Mary know that I had called and Reba said that she would.

Everything was running through my mind on why Mary is not calling me back. Is Reba not telling her that I called? Has Mary found someone else? Was Mary getting cold feet about us getting married? What was it? I had no earthly idea, but I was going to find out. That was for sure! I had to know why she was not calling me back.

I decided to postpone my visit to my grandmother to go see if I could find out what was going on. I went to Mary's parents' home, knocked on the door, and ask to speak to Mary. I was told that she wasn't there by her mother. There was something wrong here because Mary's car was in the driveway. Either she had gone somewhere with someone or she was at home. If Mary was at home then Reba was covering for her. I didn't know what was going on but I was hoping that we were just missing one another. Maybe Mary had been so busy with school that she was distracted and had forgotten the messages that her mother had given her. Yeah, right!

After that trip to Oxford I tried calling Mary several more times over the ensuing weeks with no success. I finally realized that Mary had moved on without me. Why, I did not know. I decided that I must do the same.

The problem with me moving on was that I was like a ship without a compass. I had no idea what to do. Mary had been my all and now she was gone. Damn her for doing this to me. It would have been different if I had done something hateful or mean that had caused her to leave. But that never happened.

I looked back several times a month over the next year and wondered what I did to drive Mary away. Meaningful relationships meant nothing anymore.

All I wanted to do was to see how many girls/women that I could be with. That was all I cared or thought about. I felt that all women were capable of hurting me and would probably do the same thing that Mary had done, if given the chance. Make promises and then get cold feet and leave.

I never let myself truly fall in love with another person for a long, long, long time because I did not want to have my heart broken again. Broken hell! It was shattered. Mary was the "first true love of my life" and now she was gone. I realized then that "life is a bitch more times than not."

Chapter Thirteen

Prior to 1983 I saw Mary only one other time. That was at a fraternity party and she was singing in a band. I was there with Lisa, the girl that I was dating at the time. Lisa's father had taken over the company that I was working for in Corinth. Lisa was Canadian, and her father had asked me to show Lisa around the booming metropolis of Corinth when she arrived the summer of 1982. Lisa and I got along very well and before long we were dating. I even talked her into finishing her degree at Ole Miss.

So that particular weekend at Ole Miss, Lisa and I had decided to go and listen to different bands that were playing at the fraternity houses. We ended up at the Sigma Chi house, because I still knew a ton of guys from Corinth that were in the fraternity.

When we entered the frat house the voice that I heard sounded familiar. I looked toward the stage and knew immediately that the girl singing was Mary… the Mary that once was my Mary!

With us being way in the back away from the stage I was unable to get her to see me. All I wanted to do was to say hello and asked how she had been. The song that Mary was singing seemed to be over so quickly that before I could think straight Mary was gone again. I never saw Mary's face again until the summer of 1983.

In 1983 the United States Football League was in its inaugural season and Pitt, Pitt's pop Big Ronnie, and I were planning on going to see the Memphis Showboats play at Memphis Memorial Stadium. I had called Pitt earlier in the week to see if he and his dad wanted to come over. My dad, Marcus, thought The USFL, as it was referred to, was not "really" football but a watered down version. He decided to stay in Corinth.

When Big Ronnie and Pitt arrived, we decided to get something to eat before heading to the game. We went to Overton Square in Memphis and decided on TGI Friday's. Once we were finished with our lunch it was off to the game. Little did I know that I would see someone who I had not seen since she was singing in a band at the Sigma Chi house. This would make me happy as well as sad. The real sad part had occurred earlier the week before the game.

For whatever reason I had encountered Mary's mother, Reba and sister Cindy, at Hickory Ridge mall in Memphis. They were there shopping for nothing in particular, I suppose, but who knows. When I saw them I walked up and spoke and asked how everyone was doing, especially Mary.

I will never forget the words that Mary's mother said to me because they cut through me like a knife going through hot butter. Reba said, "Everyone is fine and Mary got married." I thought, "Mary got WHAT?" I told Mary's mother to give her my best and to wish her well for me. Then I said goodbye to them and walked away.

I was hurt, sad, heartbroken, mad, pissed, and everything else you could imagine. How could or would she do this to me? We had not spoken in some time but it wasn't for the lack of me trying. Yeah, I probably had given up in my brain but I still loved her in my heart and probably always would. Now she had gone and married some guy, so my opportunity to try and get her back was gone forever!

The more I thought about what Reba had said the angrier I became. How could she do this to me? Mary and I were supposed to get married. I knew who it was! No doubt it was the guy that Mary had dated when I met her. That was who Mary had married!

Pitt, Big Ronnie, and I got to the game and the tickets we had were actually pretty good seats. We were on about the forty yard line about thirty rows up, which made it convenient to get to the restrooms should we need to go.

We watched the first quarter, and Pitt and I decided that we wanted something to drink. Big Ronnie said that he didn't want anything, so Pitt and I headed out to get some refreshments.

Pitt and I had been out on the concourse for maybe a minute at the most when Pitt says, "Isn't that Mary what's-her-name coming toward us?" I turned and said, "I believe it is." But there was something different about her. Suddenly it occurred to me that Mary had cut her hair very short! No more of the beautiful long flowing hair that I remembered, but she was still as beautiful as ever.

As Mary approached I noticed out of the corner of my eye that there was a guy headed our way along with Mary but from a different direction. I had no idea who this guy was. I had never seen him before, but apparently he knew Mary too.

Once Mary got to where Pitt and I were standing, the guy who had been closing in arrived thirty seconds later. Mary had just finished speaking to the both of us when she said, "Mike, Ronnie I would like for the two of you to meet my husband Greg." Being the gentleman I am, I extended my hand and said, "Nice to meet you Greg. I think congratulations are in order for the both of you." That was difficult to say but, hey, life goes on. He got "my girl" and I was left with nothing but the memories that we created. Win some, lose some, some get rained out, and some never get played. In this case "I was on the losing end!"

When the game was over I saw Mary one last time before we left the stadium. She smiled and waved at me and when she went out of sight I was sure that would be the last time that I would ever see her again. But you never know what will happen in the future because I believe that God does things for a reason. I think that sometimes he won't let us know our future because we are incapable of handling it. He wants us to learn from the past, live in the present, and strive toward the future.

I knew that the present was going to be very difficult for me. I would have no future with Mary, because she was now a married woman. No longer was she "my girl" but someone else's wife.

As I alluded to early, all that I did was drift from one woman to another. Sometimes I was juggling three at one time. I didn't care. There would be no long lasting love for me. I would go through life as single man because my "one true love" was gone forever.

As the years went by I never saw or heard from Mary again. The only time that I knew anything about her was at the Memphis airport in 1990 changing my ticket when I heard a voice… a voice that I had heard no telling how many times over the years that Mary and I dated. The voice that I heard was that of Riki, Mary's dad. He was somewhere close by and I had to find him. I had to find him to ask about Mary! Even though she was married I had to know that she was Ok. She was still my "first one true love" and I needed to make sure that everything was going well with her.

I continued to listen as closely as possible to make sure that I found that voice before it stopped. All at once I saw Riki standing at the ticket counter and walked up behind him. I waited until he was finished with the ticket agent and when he turned around he knew immediately who I was.

"Hi Riki, remember me?" I said. And Riki replied, "Mike, how have you been?" We shook hands and he asked what I was doing as well as how I was doing. I proceeded to tell him that I was working for a Swiss-German company and traveling the United States as well as Canada as a Sales Manager.

Quickly the conversation turned to Mary. I inquired about her, asking how she was, where she was, etc., etc. Riki told me that she was now living in California. She had three children, two boys and a girl. I remember telling Riki, "Please make sure that you tell Mary hello for me. Also tell her that I wish nothing but the best for her and her family." Riki said that he would be happy to do that.

As I walked toward security I started thinking about the first time that Mary and I met. This made me very sad knowing that we had been so, so happy at one time. Hopefully now Mary was happy. I didn't know if I would ever be happy again, though.

I could not wait to board the plane to have a beverage to try and get my mind off of Mary and what we could have had. Fate had dealt me a blow that I did not know if I could or would recover from.

Chapter Fourteen

Y ou know how I said earlier in a previously that I believe that God does not allow us to know our future because we cannot cope with it. Well, based on what happened to Mary and me, I believe it more now than ever before. There are tragedies and tragic events. Mary and I were a part of tragic events.

The following is what was related to me, not what I know. I am trying to look at it logically based on what Doctor Art said when I told the story to him. He is the psychiatrist who played a big part in my life.

The tragic event that Mary had to deal with came to a conclusion on January 31, 2007, with the death of her husband. Greg had been hitting the bottle and taking prescription drugs for a while and was on a downward spiral. When someone gets that way, no matter who you are wife, child, parent or friend-- it is impossible to bring that person back.

The booze and the pills take "total control" of their life and that is all that they care about. Unfortunately, for Mary and her children, Greg made a poor choice one night with the booze and pills.

No matter how the death of a loved one happens under those circumstances, someone always tries to place or assume blame when in all actuality the blame needs to be placed on the person or the disease that caused that person to lose his or her life.

Mary, to her credit, tried over and over to help her husband because she loved him. They had been married for almost twenty-five years, had three beautiful kids: Riki the oldest, Lauren the middle, and Kelly the youngest. But as I said earlier when something that strong has hold of you, all reasoning goes out the window and usually ends in death, either accidentally or on purpose. Maybe they don't mean to harm themselves, but they need a little more and that little more is what inevitably takes their life.

When Mary had finally had enough of Greg's abuse of alcohol and pills she gave him an ultimatum: "Either stop the abuse of your body and come back to me and the kids or I'm leaving." Well, apparently Greg did not think that Mary would actually leave him. He had been doing this for a few years, and Mary had never left before. Mary, being a strong willed person, did what she thought was best for all concerned, especially her children. She left! In Mary's mind tough love was what might snap Greg out of this downward spiral so he would come back to her and their kids.

Unfortunately for Mary, Riki, Lauren, and Kelly, that did not happen. On January 31, 2007, while Mary was on a business trip in Florida she received a call from Kelly stating, "We cannot find dad anywhere and he is not answering his phone." Kelly had actually been at the house earlier that day to pick up some clothes for basketball practice. Greg was in bed, and Kelly thought that he was sleeping. This was told to Mary by Riki, the eldest son, several months after Greg's death. Unfortunately, Greg was asleep, but this was a sleep that he would not awaken from.

Mary was in her hotel room talking to the paramedics asking, "Is he alive" hoping and praying that he was. They finally replied: "We are very sorry Mrs. Johnson; we were unable to revive him."

At that moment I am sure that Mary's world turned upside down! Mary was now a widow who had to continue to raise her three kids by herself. She now had to be both the mom and dad.

This was going to be very difficult on Mary, who for the most part of her married life had been a stay at home mom. This is not easy to do when you are in mourning and depressed, thinking that the world has fallen in on you and not knowing where to turn for help.

Depression is the first thing that sets in when someone close to you dies from anything, much less something that could have been avoided entirely. You want to do nothing; you want to see no one; talk to no one; all you want is to be left alone to grieve and ask yourself over and over, "What could I have done different to have prevented this?"

People tend to cast blame on the person left behind in a lot of instances. They feel and believe that the one left behind is not the one that should be still there, but the one who died should still be there. Why that is I do not know. What I do know is that people say hateful and cruel things sometimes because that is the only way that they know how to deal with a loss.

Several months later, after experiencing much depression Mary finally realized that it was her and her kids against the world, so to speak. She decided that life had to go on for the sake of her children. So Mary set out to make sure that she would and could support children as well as herself. This was probably the hardest thing that Mary every thought that she would have to do in her life. But as my mother always said, "Where there is a will, there is a way," Mary found both. Her will was strong and she found the way to succeed in what was needed to do keep going for her kids and herself.

Chapter Fifteen

Rhonda and I met in January 1985 at an Ob/Gyn's (Obstetrics and Gynecology) office, where she was the lead nurse. I was a pharmaceutical sales representative and the doctor that Rhonda was working for had recently been added to my territory. If not for that then we may never, have met.

It was a Friday afternoon and I had been delivering an informative gift to all of the OB's, which was what we drug reps called them. I began delivering the informative gifts to the doctors in my territory that morning and continued until my last stop which was Rhonda's office.

The meeting with Rhonda on that particular day almost didn't happen. It was cold, I was tired of being a delivery boy, and I wanted to finish up early, go to the apartment to change into my Levi's, then head to Houlihan's for a brewski before I went to pick up Cathy later that evening for our date.

When I entered the office there was Jackie the receptionist at the window where she always was. I had been to this particular OB's office a total of four times previously, so I knew Jackie and she knew me somewhat.

I would later find out the Jackie didn't like me initially because she thought I was abrasive. I thought that was ironic, since she was a Yankee and most Yankees are abrasive. Ninety nine point nine percent of us southerners, especially the men are very nice and respectful.

As it turned out on the initial meeting with Jackie, she had been yelled at that day by one of the doctors in the office. Jackie apparently was pissed at men in general the day I entered, so she was comparing me to the doctors that she worked for, as Rhonda would relate to me later.

I spoke to Jackie informing her that I had something for the doctors. I then asked if it would be Ok for me to leave it at the nurses' station. Jackie normally said that I would have to wait to see them, but apparently there was a lull in their schedules and she said, "That would be fine. See Rhonda and give her what you have for the doctors. She should be at the nurses' station." I thanked Jackie and proceeded to the back of the office toward the nurses' station. Since I had been there before, as I mentioned earlier, I knew exactly where to go.

On my way toward the nurses' station I thought, "So, the little blonde's name is Rhonda, hum?" I had caught a few glimpses of her on previous visits but I never knew her name. For that matter we had never been properly introduced. I knew that she was blonde and petite, but I never got a really good look at her face.

I proceeded to the nurses' station as Jackie had told me to do. When I got there, there was no one around and I started to leave the information for the doctors along with a note, then head out the door.

Suddenly I heard a door close and Rhonda was walking down the hall from one of the examining rooms. Man, was I taken by surprise! This Rhonda girl was very, very cute and I thought to myself, "Michael, you need to be on your best behavior with this girl and maybe, just maybe, you and she might hit it off one day."

When Rhonda had arrived at the nurses' station I extended my hand, which she shook as I was saying, "Hi, I'm Michael with Syntex and I have some informative gifts for the doctors." Rhonda responded by saying, "If you will please leave them on the counter, and I will give them to the doctors later."

Hum, I thought, she didn't tell me her name, but I was able to read it on her name tag before she wheeled around and headed off to another examination room.

You remember previously that I said that sometimes my mouth goes in motion before my brain is in gear. Well, it happened again and the best behavior thought which I had earlier went flying out the door when I uttered the following: "Ok, I would appreciate that very much. If the doctors do like the informative gifts, then I will let you buy me a drink sometime." She turned her head and looked at me like I was crazy as she was about to enter the examination room. While looking at me she shook her head and rolled her eyes, then entered.

I am standing there thinking that this highly intelligent nurse must think that I am the dumbest asshole that she had ever met, to say something like that. With that I proceeded back toward the waiting room, told Jackie goodbye, and left the office.

On the drive home I was thinking that this woman was very attractive and I would really like to go out with her. Well those chances were slim and none now, considering what I had just said. Especially the way that Rhonda had looked at me after my "open mouth, insert foot" statement only a few moments ago.

Actually she was someone that I would like to get to know. I hadn't dated anyone seriously since Mary, but I thought that Rhonda might be a possibility. Oh, I had dated over the past years, but mostly it was for a brief moment. After I had been out with them three or four times then I was finished. Kinda had a bad taste in my mouth about getting deeply involved with another woman and getting dumped again.

Not a chance in hell, would this gorgeous blonde bombshell would want to go out with me. Little did I know that another encounter was forthcoming in the not too distant future. Actually, it would be only four hours before we would see each other again.

Chapter Sixteen

I walked out the office that Friday afternoon and headed home. On the way I was trying to decide where Cathy and I would go for dinner. I wanted to make sure that I took Cathy somewhere nice. I had met Cathy a few months earlier through a friend, and we had hit it off somewhat.

Upon arriving at Houlihan's around five and the place was packed, to say the least. This was the hangout that all business people went to, especially on a Friday afternoon. The line outside would be a very long one, I thought, as I made my way to the front, greeted the hostess, Jill, whom I knew, and proceeded inside. How I went to the head of the line without waiting will be revealed later on.

About two hours later it was time to go get Cathy for our date. I said goodbye to my friends, paid my tab, and headed out the door. Upon exiting I immediately noticed Rhonda and a friend of hers standing in the cold waiting to get inside. I would later find out the Rhonda's friend's name was Pam; they had been friends since childhood.

You remember that I said that when I got to Houlihan's initially that I walked to the head of the line and entered? Well at Houlihan's, if you were a card carrying member then you could present your card and walk right in. I was a card carrying member which had assisted me earlier that evening and it was about to assist me again.

Even though Rhonda had been somewhat rude earlier, I thought what the hell, be nice, and get them in out of the cold. As I approached them it ran through my mind whether Rhonda would remember me. She hadn't really paid that much attention except when I said, "I'll let you buy me a drink if the doctors like what I brought." Would she remember what I looked like? If she didn't then all I would have to say that I was the guy with Syntex and I am sure she would remember then.

When I got to where she and her friend were standing, Rhonda noticed me immediately. The look on her face was, "Oh no! Here comes that asshole that was just in my office." When I greeted them, they were both pleasant but somewhat standoffish. As I inquired if they would like for me to get them in, both of their moods changed considerably. Rhonda said, "That would be great if you can and don't mind." My reply was, "Your wish is my command Madam. After what I said earlier this afternoon, it is the least that I can do. Follow me."

The three of us walked to the front of the line. I told Jill, the hostess, that Rhonda and her friend were with me and we walked right in. I was glad that I had one of those "hard" to come by Houlihan's cards.

I asked Rhonda how long they had been waiting and she said, "At least fifteen minutes, if not longer." If I had not happened along there is no telling how long they would have waited outside. I now was Rhonda's "Knight in Shining Armor" or at least I hoped that I was.

Once we were inside I decided to stay a little longer to see if I could talk with Rhonda, you know, maybe get to know her a little better. Rhonda did not know that was my intention I am sure by the way she reacted when I sat down with them at their table. But being a "Knight in Shining Armor" definitely has its advantages. I had saved them from the cold, and now I was about to buy their first round of drinks, little did they know. I was in like "Flint" or was I?

The waitress arrived and took our drink order. Rhonda and Pam ordered white Zinfandel, and I had another brewski. When our waitress returned with our drinks Rhonda and Pam pulled out their money and I told both Rhonda and Pam that the first round was on me. I followed that up with, "I hope that the doctors will like what I left for them today." Rhonda said, "Thank you for our drinks but you didn't have to do that." I stated that it was my pleasure and Rhonda immediately said, "I will make sure that they read and use what you left today." I smiled and said, "Thank you very much. I need all the help that I can get since this job is still very new to me."

Time seemed to fly by while I was sitting there talking to Rhonda and before I knew it I was running late for my date with Cathy. I decided to call Cathy, fabricate a story and tell her that I would be there later. Bear in mind that this was way before cell phones so I had to go use a pay phone out in the entrance area.

I excused myself from the table and headed toward the pay phone booth. While on the phone calling Cathy, I decided to tell her that Kevin was in jail. Kevin had been the person that introduced me to Cathy, so why not use him in this elaborate ruse to put Cathy off for a while so I could continue to talk to Rhonda?

While I was waiting for Cathy to answer the phone, I looked out through the glass of the phone booth and noticed Rhonda dancing with someone. I was slightly pissed that she was dancing with someone other than me, even though I had just met her that afternoon, but I was still pissed. It looked like the guy she was dancing with was shorter than she was which I thought was slightly funny.

As the phone is ringing the thought running through my mind was, "I don't have a chance with Rhonda." Here she was an attractive, highly qualified nurse and I was a lowly drug representative. Even though that previous thought was still fresh in my mind, I knew that I would have to find out if Rhonda and Michael might be a possibility. Maybe not tonight, but I would have to find out!

Cathy answered and I immediately begin the concocted story. I was kidding myself when I thought that what I was doing was Ok, because in my mind it was a "little white lie." Hell NO! There was nothing little about my lie to Cathy, plain and simple. I was standing up one girl to pursue another and this was something that I had never done before. NEVER! But at that particular moment Rhonda was all that I could really think about.

Cathy said, "Ok, is there anything that I can do?" I told her that there wasn't. I would take care of it and then head to her apartment. Cathy then caught me off guard when she said "Your ass had better be there by ten o'clock! If it isn't then don't bother coming at all because I won't be here." I said that there would be no way that I wouldn't make ten o'clock. I hung up the phone and went back to the table where Pam was because Rhonda was still on the dance floor with the little guy.

While sitting at the table and watching Rhonda dance, I was stunned by how she looked. She was five feet, two inches tall, and weighed maybe ninety-nine pounds, with blonde curly hair and wearing a black jumpsuit with the back cut out. Man was she hot and I knew, then and there, that I was going to be the one to get her. Not just for a dance or two but Rhonda was going to be my girl! Hell, maybe Rhonda will be the one that will be my wife? You never know what will happen in the future, do you?

When Rhonda returned I told her that I had to leave because I was late for my date. Why I said that I had a date was to see what her response would be. Rhonda said, "Ok and thanks again for getting us inside as well as buying our drinks." I told the both of them that they were welcome and proceeded to make my way out the door.

As I was walking out, I knew that I would have my work cut out for me with Rhonda if I wanted to make her like me, much less go out with me. With anything you have to give it your all and that was what I intended to do with Rhonda.

Earlier in the evening I had asked Rhonda for her phone number which she freely gave. She also had stated that she lived with her parents. Kinda strange to be living with your parents when you're an adult, but who am I to judge. At least I had my starting point and I would begin to pursue Rhonda the following morning. I was going to make sure that eventually I would get Rhonda out on a date. I wanted to show her that I was a "true gentleman" and then convince her to be "my girl."

Chapter Seventeen

When I arrived at Cathy's that night I was ten minutes late. Cathy, being true to her word, was not there. I was somewhat pissed because never in my wildest imagination did I believe that Cathy would not be there when I arrived. She had always been there when I was late, but not tonight. I decided to head back to Houlihan's and see if I could talk, dance, or whatever with Rhonda. So off I went to pursue Rhonda!

When I re-entered Houlihan's the place was really cranked up and I spotted Rhonda on the dance floor again. She was with the same little twerp that I had seen her dancing with earlier. I was steaming that this attractive woman would be caught dead with this little idiot. Rhonda noticed I had returned when they were finished and waved me over to their table. I sat down with her and Pam and I proceeded to expound all of the bullshit that I could muster to see if there was some interest on her part.

Rhonda asked me why I was back and I told her the truth. "I got stood up, but I was late for my date," was what I said. To which she replied, "I would have done the same thing if it had been me." I immediately knew that if I wanted to ask her out and she accepted then

I better not be late. A few moments later I asked Rhonda to dance, and this is when I truly made a fool of myself.

Since I was feeling no pain and throwing all caution into the wind, I did something that Rhonda and I would talk about over the years when we told people how we met. Never thought that would happen from the "look" I got, but we did.

You remember that I said that Rhonda's jumpsuit had the back cut out of it? Well, when Rhonda turned and she had her back to me I decided to lick up her back. There is one and only one explanation why I did this and it was the alcohol! No doubt about that!

Rhonda immediately whirled around. Should she slap me, kick me, or try to kill me? If looks could kill then I would have died on the dance floor of Houlihan's that night. Rhonda headed for our table before the dance was over. Once we were back at the table Rhonda immediately jumped all over me verbally. I tried to apologize which did no good, so I paid my tab and left.

The following morning once I had awakened I decided to give Rhonda a call. When she answered and didn't hang up on me immediately I thought that maybe she might eventually go out with me.

We talked for awhile and I could tell by the tone of her voice that she had also gotten somewhat hammered last night. Well, that made two of us, now didn't it. Who in their right mind would lick a girl's back, especially since he had only "really" known her for about six hours? No sober person would, but apparently a drunken idiot like me would.

Normally, when I would ask a girl out, if she declined two consecutive times then I knew that she really didn't want to go out in the first place and I would move on. This was not the case with Rhonda. She had plans for the next three weekends so I was already past my limit, but I asked about the fourth weekend and she said Ok. That was the beginning of our relationship that turned in to a marriage of almost nineteen years that lasted until her death.

Chapter Eighteen

Rhonda and I married in May of 1990. We had been together since February, 1985. I was working for Jostens as a recruiting and training manager at the time when we decided that it was time to tie the knot. As I mentioned earlier, Rhonda was a nurse and physician assistant at an Ob/Gyn's office. Rhonda took pride in everything that she did for "her" patients, as she referred to them.

We decided to elope. I told Rhonda that we would go wherever she wanted to go to get married. My parents had eloped and Rhonda's parents had eloped as well.

This was Rhonda's second marriage so she didn't want a church wedding again and neither did I. Rhonda had been married for about six months the first time, and it had ended very badly.

Rhonda asked me what I wanted to do. I said, "Dear it is totally up to you. We can go just about anywhere in the world with all of the frequent flyer miles I have and stay for at least a week at any Marriott, so I want you to pick our wedding location."

Rhonda chose Hawaii for our destination to become husband and wife. I immediately started getting the logistics together as well as the room.

Since I was traveling 99% of the time, we were able to fly first class via Delta because of the "Flying Colonel" status I held as well as all of the frequent flyer points I had amassed. We also had gotten a suite at the Marriott in Maui with my Marriott points. We even had a free rental car for the time we were there, from Hertz. Marriott provided dinner coupons for some of the nicest restaurants in the hotel area.

Rhonda and I were ready to start our life together and it seemed like an added "plus" that this wasn't even going to cost us very much money! So many people spend way too much money in my opinion on weddings and we were doing it the "inexpensive" way.

This all sounded so simple but in all actuality it wasn't. You see, we were going to be in Maui on a holiday week, Memorial Day to be exact, and everything was booked. Or so I was told initially. Once I inquired as to how many first class seats were still available and was informed that there were at least fifteen, tons of first class seats on an L-1011, then I was irate that we were not allowed on any of the flights. After climbing the ladder at Delta and informing them that I patronized them when it was more economical for me to fly someone else, they waved the restrictions and we were able to fly first class on the days that we wanted. My "Flying Colonel" status assisted in this endeavor as well.

The Marriott on Maui was a lot easier. I had to call the hotel and talk with the manager. I informed him that Rhonda and I wanted to get married on their property, the day after Memorial Day, which was May 29th, and he said they were more than willing to accommodate us.

The wedding was simple in that the only witnesses that we had was the photographer who took our wedding photos and one of the bellmen. We did have an audience up above on the balconies of some of the rooms because I remember the applause that we received when we kissed after the minister said, "I now pronounce you husband and wife."

We were in Hawaii for over a week and enjoyed every minute of it there. Leaving Hawaii was difficult, but we had to come back to reality. We had to go back to work as husband and wife now, making a happy life for one another.

Rhonda would return to Methodist North, in the Memphis metro area, where she was now working, and I would return to Jostens at my recruiting and training manager position. We would be together for the rest of our lives. At least I thought that we would.

Chapter Nineteen

With everything that Rhonda had going for her, unfortunately she also had something really bad going against her. Rhonda had OCD, Obsessive Compulsive Disorder, which caused her to count everything she did over and over.

I knew that Rhonda was afflicted with this condition when we became involved but I had no idea that it was as bad as it turned out to be. Rhonda did whatever she could to hide her compulsion because she thought that it made her look stupid or crazy, which was far from the truth.

Rhonda had finished second in her nursing class. She would say that she should have finished first. The only reason that she hadn't was that a lady, who was older than her by about fifteen years, had been "given" the valedictorian honors because of her age. Rhonda would tell me, "I should have been the valedictorian because I know that I was cheated by my professor." This was probably not far from that truth, because Rhonda had a Mensa I.Q. When it came to medical information, then I had rather trust her than most of the doctors that I knew! Rhonda was also a P.A. (Physicians Assistant) and this took considerable amount of time, with both the studying along with the hands on work, to achieve this level of expertise.

Rhonda worked her little butt off until I got a break with an offer that we could not refuse. The offer would take us to Dallas, Texas, in 1997 for a sales job with a converting paper company. This company sold paper rolls as well as sheeted printing paper to publishers and printers throughout the United States.

Once we were settled in Irving, Texas, Valley Ranch to be exact, I told Rhonda that if she didn't want to work then that was OK with me.

I had noticed that her OCD was getting progressively worse before we moved to Texas. I wanted her to be able to relax and not have any undue stress if it was possible. The position that I now had would allow me to pay all the bills and still save some money. We didn't need for Rhonda to work to make ends meet, and this suited her fine. She would now be able to relax, take care of the townhouse and do some girlie things.

Rhonda decided to take me up on the offer of not working. The reduced stress from not having to take care of patients seemed to allow her OCD to subside when she stopped working. For a couple of years the OCD seemed to be almost non-existent. But when it did reappear it came back with a vengeance.

From 1997 until 2002 everything was pretty good for Rhonda and me. My job was going great and the raises were coming frequently. We leased a new car for Rhonda and we were also saving money for our retirement.

In 2002 things started to change for the worse. Rhonda's primary care physician moved to Arizona. This bothered her immensely because this was one doctor that she actually believed in and trusted.

Before he moved he asked Rhonda if she would like to have her records. Since she was a nurse, even though not a practicing one since 1997, she knew that it might be a good idea to have them just in case something arose.

Well something more than arose one night while she was looking at her records. It actually devastated the both of us. While reading over her medical records, Rhonda said, "Michael, it states here that I have a brain tumor." My immediate response was, "What did you just say?" I knew what I had heard but I really couldn't believe what had registered in my brain at the moment that those words cut into it like a knife. That is why I asked her to repeat what she had just said. She replied once again, "I have a brain tumor!"

We both sat there and looked at one another in disbelief. This information had come from a neurologist. He had done a CT scan along with an MRI (Magnet Resonance Imaging) on Rhonda a couple of years back. Rhonda had started having severe headaches and seizures back around that time. She had finally relented, going see a neurologist at my request.

Since Rhonda was a little girl she had been having seizures. Each and every dumbass doctor that her parents had taken her to had said that she was epileptic. Well, back in the days that Rhonda and I were adolescents, there was no such thing as an MRI. Hell, I don't even know if CT scans were available back then. Maybe all that we had back then was an x-ray machine? If the x-ray didn't show anything then as far as all dumbass doctors knew everything was alright.

I was as almost as bad as Rhonda when it came to doctors. Even now, I very rarely go to a doctor for anything except a physical. I am still somewhat concerned that they will make a mistake or miss something during the physical that they should have seen.

But how do you miss a brain tumor? The radiologist had read the CT scan as well as the MRI. He had made notations on the report and all the neurologist had to do was to read what had been written. To me, what was done to Rhonda was downright cruel. Most doctors, not all of them mind you, thought of themselves as gods. If the truth be known, several of them are, were and forever will be "dumber than dirt!"

I was stunned, appalled, and mortified that the asshole neurologist had said absolutely nothing about finding a tumor. Who knows why that happened? I certainly don't but I pray to God that there is a special hell for him when he dies!!!!!

Immediately I got on the computer and began researching this tumor. I found out that it was one of the rarest tumors in the world. Rhonda had a Colloid tumor of the third ventricle, a rare benign intracranial non-neoplastic cystic tumor.

Colloid cyst tumors of the third ventricle are a rare cause of headache and sudden death. Approximately three persons per million per year are affected by this entity. This comes to .000005%, which to me is very rare indeed.

Over the years that we had not known about the tumor was that it had grown from 7 centimeters to 37 by the time we found out. That to me is a pretty quick growing tumor.

Now with that being said, I know that Rhonda would have probably not let anyone cut on her brain no matter what. But since we had not been informed properly, Rhonda never had the opportunity to make that decision.

Rhonda had become terrified of doctors. The only one that she trusted was her primary care physician and Dr. Art, her psychiatrist. Rhonda's favorite saying was, "Michael, do you know why they call it practicing medicine? Because they never can get it right the first time so they have to keep practicing!"

A few years earlier there was an instance when Rhonda was admitted to the hospital for kidney stones. She was in extreme pain and to combat that pain the attending physician gave her morphine. The second night that Rhonda was in the hospital, I was home trying to sleep. Rhonda called, mumbling for me to come to the hospital. I barely could understand her because she was slurring her words. My first thought was "Oh no, Rhonda is having a seizure."

I rushed out of the townhouse and flew to the hospital. I was fortunate that the police didn't stop me, but at that time I wouldn't have cared. Something was wrong and I had to get to Rhonda in a hurry.

When I entered Rhonda's room there was blood all over the floor as well as all over Rhonda and the bed. I asked her what happened. With her still slurring her words I was able to make out the following; "The pump malfunctioned. I pulled out the I.V."

If that had been you or me or anyone else we would have died from a morphine overdose. Because of Rhonda's medical background, she was able to save her own life. As usual, the medical staff had no idea how or why this happened. This is just another example why Rhonda had become frightened of doctors and hospitals.

Through the years after discovering the tumor, Rhonda went to the hospital numerous times. We would be out to dinner and she would have a seizure; an ambulance would be called, and off we would go to the hospital. This became frustrating to Rhonda as well as to me. An ambulance trip to the hospital and nothing was done to help her. The ER docs might give her some Ativan or Xanax to control the seizure. As the old saying goes, "If you throw enough crap on the wall, eventually something is going to stick." And that was all that they ever tried to do!

I remember one instance in 2007 when Rhonda had a seizure at the local watering hole we frequented. The ambulance was summoned and once we were at the hospital, the doctor told me as well as Rhonda that she was faking her seizure. It was all that I could do to keep from whipping his ass for that bizarre statement. We knew then and there that doctors were idiots. What medical doctor that supposedly adheres to the Hippocratic Oath would even say such a thing. The reason that he said what he had uttered was he had no frigging idea what he was supposed to do!

The seizures were becoming more and more frequent causing Rhonda to withdraw more and more from society. Initially Rhonda would maybe get out of the house two to three times per week. She would go to a movie or go to the mall to window-shop. On occasions Rhonda would go to our local hangout and wait for me to get off of work to meet her there.

Steadily though, the times Rhonda would leave the townhouse went down considerably. It went from two to three times a week to one time a week then to twice a month and then to never.

Rhonda went eight weeks in 2007 without ever walking outside our townhouse. That is two whole months, damn it!

All she ever wanted to do during that time was to watch TV, rent movies or sitcoms, eat, and sleep. Her favorite sitcoms were "Friends" and "Everybody Loves Raymond." I bet that Rhonda had watched each and every episode of those two sitcoms no fewer than ten times each. It got to the point that I knew what they were going to say or do because I had watched them with her to keep her company.

I was beginning to get very worried about Rhonda. Dr. Art, who was Rhonda's psychiatrist, was getting worried as well. Rhonda thought that the medications that she was on needed to be decreased. She would often tell me, "Michael, if I had never taken any of this crap to begin with, then maybe I would be better than I am today." I wouldn't nor could I disagree with her. I knew that Rhonda was living in hell on earth, with all that she was going through.

I had no idea what her life would be like without the medication. What I did know was that she was living in total hell and the medications were not helping or they had stopped helping. I had never seen anyone, much less been around anyone whose will was any stronger than Rhonda's. Rhonda would always say to me that "She wanted to be normal. But what's normal, Michael?"

Rhonda decided that she wanted to decrease her medication for the seizures. Her thought was that the medication had stopped working and she would be better off by not taking anything or at least reducing it substantially. No use in trying to talk her out of this because when Rhonda wanted to do something, then she did it.

Through this difficult time for Rhonda, I tried to make it as easy on her as possible. I did the grocery shopping, vacuumed, cleaned, and anything else that would make her life easier.

While doing this for my wife, some of my "so called friends" would say, "Why don't you leave her?" My reply would be, "I got married for life. Rhonda has stood by me and therefore there is no way in hell I am not going to stand by her"!

Chapter Twenty

Everything started to get worse in April of 2008. I was supposed to come home by eleven to take Rhonda to the dentist. Two to three months previously Rhonda had gotten into the old Mitsubishi that we owned and had driven to the movies. She had decided that I was not getting ready quick enough and took off on her own. She made it to the movie Ok, but when she left the theater she had a seizure.

Rhonda wrecked the car. Approximately twenty eight hundred dollars of damage was done. Two tires had been blown out when she hit the curb; two rims were damaged as well and the left front fender was just about torn off. Oh, the hub caps for the tires were no longer useable. Rhonda was Ok, thank god, but after that accident we decided that she never needed to drive again. Since Rhonda was no longer driving I came home one morning to take her to the dentist. What I found upstairs in the bathroom scared the crap out of me!

I arrived home that morning at eleven because her appointment was at eleven thirty. As I entered in the townhouse, climbing the stairs, I thought that I heard the water in the shower running. This was not unusual for Rhonda. She had been taking hour to hour and half showers for the past three months every day. Rhonda would say to me, "I know that I am clean but I cannot get out of the shower."

Today, though, this did seem unusual because Rhonda was about to be late for her appointment and Rhonda never wanted to be late for anything. As I ascended the stairs to the shower area I was constantly calling her name. Normally she would be responding but today she wasn't. This was scaring the hell out of me and once at the top of the stairs I knew why she wasn't answering me.

Rhonda was lying on the bathroom floor naked and wet. It looked like someone had beaten the holy hell out of her. She had bruises on her legs, her arms, her face, and she had thrown up on herself and on the bathroom floor. The first thing that I thought was that someone had broken in and done this to her. Then I remembered that the front door was locked because I had just unlocked it a few moments ago.

As I was trying to talk to her, it hit me! Rhonda must have taken something, but what? She was mumbling and rolling back and forth on the floor. She kept saying, "Let me die. Please let me die."

I ran to the bedroom and saw that all of the bottles of her medications were empty. Apparently Rhonda had fallen several times after taking all of the pills that had been at her disposal. That was why she had all of the bruises on her body.

Rhonda had taken all of her Xanax, which was two bottles of sixty each. Remember I said that she had wanted to decrease her medications. Apparently Rhonda had been planning this for some time. She also had taken two complete bottles of Tylenol PM and who knows what else. Rhonda had planned on dying that day. I am sure or at least I am relatively sure that Rhonda thought that she would be dead when I arrived that morning to take her to the dentist, but she wasn't. I felt that as long as I had anything to do with it Rhonda was not going to die!

Later I found a suicide note that she had left on the downstairs counter. It detailed the misery that she had been going through and in her mind she thought she would be better off dead.

I didn't know what to do. Do I call 911? Rhonda had told me to never ever call 911 again! She hated doctors and would not go to the frigging hospital again. So I called Dr. Art, her psychiatrist. He advised me to get her in the shower and keep a close eye on her. Dr. Art asked if Rhonda had thrown up and I said yes. Dr. Art thought that since the majority of the pills had been expelled that she would be Ok as long as I was there to take care of her. I told him that I would be there to take care of her and would not leave her side.

After helping Rhonda back into the shower, then out approximately two hours later, I put her to bed and stood watch over her throughout the night. The next morning she was irate with me because I had not let her die. I promised her that as long as I was around I would not let her die.

Unfortunately, a year and a month later when we were living in Frisco, I was unable to keep my promise to Rhonda.

Chapter Twenty One

Rhonda died on May the 8th, 2009; three weeks shy of our 19th anniversary. It was a beautiful Friday morning and I had just finished working out when I walked into the living room and Rhonda was in the kitchen. I said, "Oh you're getting in the shower." She was naked and normally she wouldn't be undressed unless she was about to get in the shower. Rhonda said, "No I am going back to bed."

This was not uncommon for Rhonda to go back to bed because for the past two years she had been sleeping about two hours a night. Rhonda was going through menopause, with the hot flashes, mood swings, -- and worst of all-- the insomnia. So for her to try and get the "much needed rest" that her body craved, was a good idea. After all, it was Friday and I would be home all day working out of my office, so I could let Zoe, our little Yorkshire terrier, out to do her business as well as whatever else that needed to be done that day.

Rhonda had made a list of things we needed from the grocery store: bread, Triscuts, and paper towels. I said, "OK, I will get the stuff on the list as soon as I get out of the shower." She said, "OK! I love you, Michael." I said, "I love you too dear."

I then headed for the shower not knowing that the words that we had just spoken would be the last words that we would ever say to one another.

As I mentioned earlier in previous chapters, Rhonda had been suffering from OCD (Obsessive Compulsive Disorder) since she was a teenager. She was also diagnosed with high anxiety, and to make matters even worse, she had an inoperable brain tumor.

On my way to get in the shower I decided that I first needed to do something that would take me about five to ten minutes for work, so I sat down at the computer. I have no idea how long I had been on the computer when all of a sudden I heard a loud pop! The sound that registered in my brain was that of a starter's pistol at a track and field event. I knew that it wasn't a starter's pistol but a real gun. It was a gun that Rhonda had since I had known her. We had kept it in a cabinet under the television stand in the bedroom. It was loaded with full metal jacket of .38 rounds.

You might ask why we had a loaded gun in the house. You have every right to ask that question, and I will try to explain. The position that I had with my company, as a Regional Sales/Market Manager, required that I travel overnight at times leaving Rhonda alone. This was unavoidable but since I was the only one capable of working, it couldn't be helped. With me not at home Rhonda wanted some sort of deterrent should anything happen. Not that we resided in a dangerous area. We actually lived in an area that was very safe, with an alarm system in our gated community. I think the gun was more for peace of mind than anything else.

I knew immediately that something bad had just happened! I took off toward the bedroom running and yelling, "No Rhonda! No Rhonda! Dear God, No Rhonda!" Zoe was whining and running around in circles. She knew that something bad had just happened. I finally corralled her and put her in her kennel.

I was in shock by the sound I had just heard! I did not know what to do. But I knew that I had to open the door and see if Rhonda was alright, but in my heart I knew that she wasn't or she would have been answering me as I was yelling her name.

The fear that I felt cannot really be put into words but I will try and explain what was coursing through my body on that Friday morning. Do you remember when you were little and you heard a sound at night while you were in bed? You were sure that there was something outside your door. You were scared to death because you were afraid of the boogie man. You would gather all of the courage that you could muster to open the door and look. Nothing there! No boogie man, nothing at all. That was how I felt on May the 8th, 2009 at 7:52, on that Friday morning.

I was hoping and praying that the gun had accidentally discharged. Rhonda would be Ok, and the reason that she wasn't answering me when I was calling her name was that she was in shock. As much as I wanted and tried to make myself believe this, I knew in my heart that would not be the case.

I had my cell phone in one hand and the land line phone in the other. I was dialing 911 and Rhonda's shrink simultaneously. I immediately hung up on both of them! What do I do?

I was trembling and crying hysterically and hoping against hope that Rhonda was OK. I finally got the courage to open the door ever so slightly, maybe an inch or so. Once I looked through the slight opening my worst fear was realized. There was Rhonda, in the bed with the gun in her hand and blood all over her little face.

I was screaming at the top of my lungs, "NO RHONDA, NO RHONDA! DEAR GOD PLEASE DON'T LET THIS BE HAPPENING!" I grabbed the land line phone and dialed 911. When the 911 operator answered I told her that my wife had just shot herself in the head. The lady dispatcher asked me to repeat myself because she said that she was having trouble understanding what I was saying. I tried to calm myself so she would understand me and when she did, I will never forget what she said to me: "Sir, I need you to go back in the room and let me know if she is still breathing."

I begged her not to ask me to do that. I did not want to see the woman that I had been married to for almost nineteen years lying in bed, with blood all over her little face again. But the 911 operator said that she needed to know if Rhonda was still breathing or not.

I reopened the door and looked at Rhonda. I told the dispatcher, "I don't see her breathing!" I had to repeat myself again because she could not understand what I was saying. I was crying uncontrollably. It seemed like at 7:52 that Friday morning I started crying and didn't stop until sometime later that afternoon.

The coroner would later tell me, "Rhonda didn't feel a thing. She left this earth before you ever left your office. She, more than likely, didn't even hear the sound of the gun discharging. In other words, 'Rhonda left this world in a twinkle of an eye'."

Chapter Twenty Two

I was waiting outside for the police to arrive as well as the
paramedics, hoping against hope that Rhonda would and could
be saved. Once the police officer got there he asked me what had
happened and where Rhonda was. I told him what had transpired and
where to find her. When he returned to where I was outside I looked
and saw the ambulance about to enter and then suddenly it turned off
its siren and headed away. I knew then, for sure, that Rhonda, my wife
for almost nineteen years, was dead! I started crying uncontrollably
and yelling "Dear God No! Dear God No!" And wondering what was
I going to do now that there is no more Rhonda in my life?

Now here I was all by myself with the exception of Zoe. I knew
that I would not be the only one affected by Rhonda's tragic death. Zoe
would be affected as well, not to mention Rhonda's immediate family.

I know most of you probably think this is crazy, but I knew that
Zoe would be looking for and missing her mommy. Rhonda had been
with Zoe from the day we got her and had never been away. Now Zoe
would be heartbroken just like I would be. I knew that Zoe would look
for her mommy continuously, wondering where she was. I decided that
I would tell her that her mommy had gone to live with God. I knew

that she wouldn't understand me, but then again who knows, maybe she did in her own little mind.

Everyone from the police department had gotten there: two detectives, four uniform officers, and the C.S.I. (Crime Scene Investigation) Unit. Everyone proceeded to asked me what happened and after repeating myself over and over again, I finally said, "Guys I have no idea if I am even making sense anymore or if I am even saying the same thing that I said the first ten times." To which one of the detectives said, "Michael we know that you had absolutely nothing to do with your wife's death. We thought that if you would talk about what happened that it might help you in some way." They asked me if there was anyone that I could call, and I said there was and immediately called Joe.

I was taken in by Joe and Susan Lappin. Without them I have no idea what I would have done. Rhonda had met Joe about eleven years previously at an Italian pizzeria. She had called me that afternoon and said, "Michael, you need to come over here and meet this guy I just met named Joe. I think the two of you will get along great because he loves to play golf as much as you do." Joe and I met that Sunday afternoon and we have been friends ever since, thanks to Rhonda's phone call. Little did I know at the time that Rhonda had introduced me to the person who would be my rock eleven years in the future.

Immediately, Joe said that he was on his way and I told him not to come until I called him back because I had no idea how long the police would be there. Then I called Pitt, my best friend, and he said that if I needed him there, he would be on the way. I told him there was no need for him to drive all that way, plus I thought that Rhonda's family would want to have a memorial service for her. I would be in Tennessee for that and maybe then he could come to the service.

I then called my brother-in-law, Mike, and told him what had happened. Mike wanted to know if I was alright and I said, "I am as good as I can be right now with all that has happened this morning. I pray that Rhonda is in a better place and she is no longer suffering."

Mike said that he would tell Kristie, Rhonda's sister, as well as be with her when they went to tell Rhonda's parents. I then called Dr. Art, who I had to leave a message for, and then my boss. My boss was very sympathetic and said that he would discuss how much time they would allow me off and to not worry about anything. He would make sure that my territory was covered.

Dr. Art called me back almost immediately. He was very concerned about my well being. He suggested that we meet over the weekend to discuss what had happened. He said that he would be in his office on Saturday and he thought that it would be a good idea for us to sit down and talk about what I had witnessed. I agreed and we scheduled to meet at twelve o'clock the next day.

Later on in the morning after I had composed myself as much as anyone can compose themselves after witnessing what I saw, I called my mom. She was so helpful in that she said, "I always thought a lot of Rhonda and hopefully she is in a better place and not suffering any longer." Mom was concerned about me as well, and I told her the Joe and Susan would take care of me which seemed to give her some solace.

Joe picked me up around twelve forty five that Friday, and I stayed with him and Susan until I flew out for the memorial service the following Monday morning. If it had not been for the Lappin family I do not know what I would have done.

Chapter Twenty Three

The memorial service for Rhonda was held in Linden, Tennessee, where Rhonda's parents lived. I flew into Nashville and my brother-in-law picked me up at the airport on Monday, May the 10th, the day after Mother's Day.

It was the first time that I had seen any of Rhonda's family in over five years. The last time that Rhonda and I had seen them had been at my father's funeral in July 2003.

The morning of the memorial service I decided that I wanted to stand up in front of those attending and let them know why Rhonda was no longer with us. I wanted those in attendance to know that Rhonda wasn't crazy. It was because she had so many demons running through her mind, with the OCD, the anxiety, plus the brain tumor, that she was not the Rhonda that we all knew and loved. I told them that Rhonda was the nicest, most giving person that I had ever known, and that the world was a better place when she was in it.

That was the second hardest thing that I have ever done in my life... for me to stand in front of an audience and speak from my heart about Rhonda while crying through each and every word.

The photos that were displayed of Rhonda brought back good memories of a time when things were better and we were happy. Oh, how I missed Rhonda. She would forever be a part of my existence.

When I returned to Frisco, Texas, from the memorial service in Linden, Tennessee, on Wednesday, I knew immediately that I had to get out of the townhouse where Rhonda had died as soon as possible. I stayed with the Lappin family a couple more nights until the townhome had been cleaned. Then I was able to go back there until another place was found for Zoe and me.

We moved out of Frisco by the middle of the following week and what a relief it was to be away from where Rhonda had died. Rhonda and I had lived in Plano before a few years back and we had been happy there. That is the reason I think that I was drawn back to that area. I was able to find a small one bedroom apartment very quickly, and that is where Zoe and I moved to.

On May the 29th, 2009, which would have been mine and Rhonda's nineteenth anniversary I took Zoe with me to a beautiful park and scattered Rhonda's ashes. That was what she had told me to do should anything happen to her. That is a day that I will not forget.

With a move comes a change of scenery, finding new places to eat, locations of new cinemas, and on and on. I knew that it would be impossible to go see a movie where Rhonda and I use to go, eat where we use to eat, or go to the mall that she liked to frequent, when I could get her out, so I stayed away from all of the places that were "ours." I had to find different places to frequent as to not bring back memories, which made me sad because Rhonda was no longer there.

Joe stayed in constant contact with me almost every day. We would play golf together or go to Gecko's, a local hangout, to watch college football on Saturday's or to watch the Dallas Cowboys on Sunday's. Gecko's was the place that Joe took me the day Rhonda committed suicide and for some reason I was always drawn back there. I loved the atmosphere and over the months I met a ton of nice people and I felt at home there.

I realized that life must go on now after Rhonda's death. I wanted Zoe to be comfortable and happy as well as me. It was Zoe and I alone together and we would have to make the best of our situation.

Chapter Twenty Four

From the time after scattering Rhonda's ashes on May the 29th, our anniversary, until October in 2009, everything is somewhat a blur.

I initially tried to go back to work. But no matter how hard I tried, it seemed that everywhere I looked, I was reminded of Rhonda. My nights were lonely, with the exception of Zoe, but as all of us know, there is no dog that will talk to you, or at least mine wouldn't.

I decided to go to Corinth for a visit in July to see my mom and my Aunt A as well as my friends. It was good to be back at "home" around people that I knew, loved, and had grown up with. Everyone that I encountered was very sympathetic to my loss and I appreciated that very much.

When I returned to Texas at the end of July, I decided that with Rhonda's suicide it was going to be difficult to continue to live anywhere in the state, much less in close proximity to where the tragedy had occurred. I met with Dr. Art on several occasions and he diagnosed me with PTSD (Post Traumatic Stress Disorder). He suggested that I move to Corinth permanently to be around people that meant a lot to me because he said that it would take time for the healing to begin after the loss of a loved one which had happened in such a tragic way.

So I called my mother and told her that I was thinking about moving back to Corinth. She said, "You are always welcome here Mike, for as long as you want to stay." I knew that would be what she would say, but I wanted to ask anyway.

The week prior to Rhonda's suicide we had discussed moving to Corinth. Rhonda said that she would and could look after my mother and in turn mom could make sure that Rhonda was Ok as well. I really wish that we had moved the week that we discussed it; then maybe Rhonda would still be here and we would be in Corinth. That wasn't to be though, but now Zoe and I were going to head home and see what happened.

We would leave on Halloween night. Can you say Trick or Treat? Well I thought that Halloween had come early on October 24th. It wasn't a trick but it was definitely a TREAT!

Chapter Twenty Five

Y ou remember that I said I believe the reason that God will not let us know our future is that we do not have the mental capacity to deal with what may be about to unfold. Well, if I had known what was about to happen that Saturday morning, October 24th, I truly do not believe that I would have a problem dealing with it at all. I just wouldn't have believed that it was possible! Everyone knows "God works in mysterious ways," and you are about to see what I mean by that.

Joe and I were supposed to meet at Gecko's on that Saturday to watch football all afternoon. My usual ritual every morning was to get a cup of coffee, then take Zoe out for her to do her "morning business." I would then fire up the computer to see what was going on in the world as I had done every morning for the past ten years.

After reading CNN news and CNN sports I usually went to AOL to check my messages. When I looked at the spam folder that morning I thought, "Wow, there is more spam than normal. What is going on today with all of this junk mail?" You would not believe all of the spam that had hit my computer; well, maybe you would, because I know that it happens to everyone, not just me. While cleaning out the spam I noticed a message that took my breath away. You see, in August I had put myself on Facebook just in case someone who didn't know where I was could find me. The "Wow" that I had initially uttered for all of the spam I received over the past night quickly turned into a "double WOW". Hell, this was probably a triple or quadruple WOW for that matter. I am reading this Facebook invite and thinking to myself, "Is this for real? Why would she be looking for me? Is this really from Mary, MY MARY?"

My next thought was what do I do? Then, how do I reply back? This was the first invite that I had had, so I was a novice about the process, believe it or not.

I decided to click on the link and immediately was taken to the page where I confirmed the invite and then I could see the photos of this mysterious Mary. Mysterious in the fact of why, after all of these years is she trying to contact me?

On her Facebook page I saw the first photo of Mary with some young adults. I knew instantly that it was definitely Mary, but I had no idea who the two boys and one girl were. Then it hit me! The three young adults must be Mary's children. I remembered my conversation with Mary's dad years ago when he had stated that Mary had three kids. This must be them! But why wasn't her husband in the photo as well? I would find that out later that morning.

I decided to respond and looked at the time on my computer. It was early, well, early for a Saturday morning anyway, around 6:15 or somewhere thereabout. I started typing and being the joker I am sometimes, I decided to send this reply: "Is this, the same Mary Yoshino that I knew at Ole Miss?" Yoshino was Mary's middle name, but she had changed the middle part of her name on the Facebook page to her maiden name. Or at least that is what I thought she had done when she married. I knew all along that it was her, but I wanted to be "absodamnlutely" sure!

I had no idea when she might respond. Was she awake now? Did she have access to a computer at this time? Where was she living? All of these thoughts were running through my mind when I hit send. Almost instantaneously the reply that I received was, "Yes, Mike it is me." When I read those words my heart skipped a beat. I had not seen, heard from, much less spoken to Mary in over twenty-six years. And now Mary was getting in touch with me! Why?

As I would find out that fateful Saturday, Mary had had a dream about me the night before. In her dream there was something tragic that had happened to me. She felt that I was hurting and that I needed to talk to someone. Mary was correct in that something tragic had happened, but why her? Did she feel a connection to me still, after all of these years apart? I didn't know, but what I did know was that I wanted to talk to Mary and the sooner, the better.

Here was the woman that I had been in love with so many years ago reaching out to me because of a dream. I was in shock to say the least that this had happened, but I was so happy that I was speechless for a moment.

Mary and I started communicating via the Internet that morning, back and forth, back and forth, until I asked for her number. I needed, wanted, and had to hear her voice again. When I heard Mary's voice it was like "old times" in that she sounded the same. Mary has a nice soothing and caring voice, and it brought back old memories… Memories of a time when things were a lot less complicated. That was a time when we were happy and in love.

Mary would later tell me, "I decided to try Facebook, knowing all along that there is no way that I will find Mike. But when I saw the Ole Miss hat on your head I knew it was you 'for sure'." Thank God for Facebook!

Mary told me about the tragic event in her life. I then told her about that had happened to Rhonda. It seemed that our lives had been parallel in nature, to a certain degree. I was thinking "how wonderful and weird" is this? Mary had lost her husband to alcohol and pills and I had lost my wife to OCD, and a brain tumor, along with anxiety that led to her suicide.

We talked, e-mailed another, texted one another, and then on one phone call I said something about maybe coming for a visit. I will never forget what Mary said. She said, "Mike you are always welcome anytime. My door is always open for you to come and visit." My reply was, "Be careful what you wish for, you may actually get it."

To be honest, I felt guilty that I wanted to go and see Mary especially since Rhonda had only died five months prior. I discussed this with Dr. Art and his exact words were, "Michael, Rhonda left you. You did not leave her. You stayed to the very end where others would have walked away, but yet you stayed. I do not know anyone else that would have done what you did." I said, "Thanks Dr. Art, but I really don't think it is the right thing to do." While I was saying those words, I did not believe what was coming out of my mouth. I had lost Mary many years ago. Why, I never knew. What I did know now was to pass up the opportunity to see her again would be utter foolishness.

As I was thinking about what Dr. Art had just said about not feeling guilty he hit me with something else. "To hear you speak of and about Mary it seems that there is and maybe always has been something there with you and her. She would have not have reached out to you if she had not been concerned for you. I believe that she has feelings for you Michael or she wouldn't have had the dream. Maybe they have been buried for all of these years and who knows why they have surfaced, but they did." The last statement was the one that really hit home with me when he said, "Do you want to run the risk of losing her to someone else, because you didn't or won't make the leap?"

Dr. Art had just said what I had been thinking. I had already decided to go see Mary; I just needed to be reassured that it was OK to do so. I did not want to disrespect the memory of Rhonda by doing something that I thought might be incorrect without first consulting someone who I trusted and who knew what I had gone through.

I have heard so many people say after a spouse died, "Well he/she sure didn't wait too long to jump back in. I can't believe it because he/she has only been dead for a short period of time." I didn't want to be one of those people. But then again I wanted, needed, and had to see Mary. If Mary's initial invitation was really true and I hoped that it was, then come "hell or high water", I was going to South Carolina to see her for the first time in over twenty-six years.

I told Joe, Susan, Pitt, and everyone else that I knew, what had happened. They were all in agreement that I should go see Mary. So I started planning for the trip to Hilton Head, South Carolina to go see "My" Mary!

Chapter Twenty Six

As I mentioned earlier, I was planning on moving back home to Corinth, Mississippi, to look after my mother because I wasn't working now. I had been put on disability by Dr. Art because of what I had seen the morning of May the 8th. He had diagnosed me with PTSD, or Post Traumatic Stress Disorder.

Dr. Art said, "Michael I cannot imagine what ran through your brain the moment you opened the door and saw Rhonda there. No one will ever be able to understand that unless they encounter the same thing." He felt that I did not need to be in the same work environment and based on how I was feeling, the dreams I was having, and various other things I was going through, the best thing for me right then was to take some time off.

Dr. Art thought that it would be a good idea for me to be around more people that I knew and loved. He knew that it would be difficult leaving Texas. After all, it had been mine and Rhonda's home for over twelve and a half years. Plus I would not be able to see Joe and Susan on a regular basis.

Mary and I continued to talk via the Internet as well as on the phone, and then I brought up the idea of taking her up on her offer to visit her. Mary told me again while we were talking on the phone, "Mike, you are more than welcome to come and visit anytime that you want. My home is always open for you, and I would love to see you again".

When Mary had finished talking that day, there was no doubt that I was going to visit her. All that was to be decided was when would be a good time. When we talked again the next day, we decided that December the 8th would be as good a time as any. This would give me time to be in Corinth with my mother for a month before I went for the visit.

Then I thought that it would be seven months to the day that Rhonda had committed suicide if I arrived on the 8th of December. This was dripping with irony here, in that Rhonda died on May the 8th and I am going to visit my "long lost love" on December the 8th. That was something that I did not wish to do because what if Mary and I hit it off again and it was on the 8th, the same 8th that Rhonda died, only a different month. Then that would not be good karma I thought. I decided, unknown to Mary that I would pick a different date and it probably would be sooner than she had anticipated.

After I had been in Corinth for week I told my mother about Mary getting in touch with me. I mentioned that I was thinking about going to visit her, and I wanted my mom's opinion. My mom means a lot to me, and I guess that I wanted her blessing before I made the trip. To me it would be much easier to go and see Mary if mom thought that it was Ok to do so.

I remember saying, "Mom I really want and need to go and visit Mary in South Carolina. I probably 'loved' her more than anyone I have ever loved in my life. She is the one that I should have married all those years ago and for whatever reason we didn't get married. What do you think about me visiting her and do you think it is too early, since Rhonda has not been gone that long?"

Mom said, "I want you to be happy and if going to see Mary will make you happy then that is what you should do." She then said, "There is no one that I could ever love as much as I loved your daddy. There is not another man alive that I would be interested in whatsoever." I knew what she was saying. Mom was saying that pop, as I called him, was her one "true" love.

Even though Rhonda and I had been married for almost nineteen years and had many happy times together, I knew that Mary was my one true love, just as Rhonda had told me that Byron had been her one true love. So I decided that I was going to see Mary and thought, South Carolina here I come!

I still knew and felt that Rhonda and I would always be connected. We had been together for twenty five years and we were three weeks shy of our nineteenth anniversary when Rhonda decided to end her pain and suffering. The more I thought about seeing Mary the more I believed that Rhonda would want me to go on with my life and be happy.

I will never forget Rhonda just as Mary will never forget Greg, but they are both gone and Mary and I are still here. We have a chance, a second chance at love. There are not too many people that are given that opportunity, and I was not going to let this pass me by.

So after the conversation with my mother and talking to Mary every day via text, Facebook, e-mail, or on the phone, we decided that I would come for a visit. We continued to talk about December the 8th being the day that I would arrive, all the time knowing that it wouldn't be that day because of the significance of the number.

As I said earlier about visiting Mary, the sooner the better and since November came before December, then why not. Why wait until December anyway? We discussed an earlier meeting and decided that I would come in on November the 12th. We both were counting the days of my arrival when I changed my mind and decided to leave a day earlier.

My decision was to leave on the 11th of November, though I was still telling Mary that I was coming in on the 12th of November. I wanted to surprise her with my early arrival and even mentioned that she might not be able to get in touch with me on the 11th because I had so many things to do to get ready for the trip.

The more that I thought about surprising her the more I decided that would not be a good thing to do, especially since I had not seen her in over twenty-six years. A friend of mine's girlfriend said that if I surprised her and she was not ready, you know hair done, nails painted, etc., it might make her uncomfortable and that was the "last" thing I wanted to do. After listening to the explanation I decided that I would tell Mary that I would be arriving a day early.

On Monday night, November the 10th, I told Mary that I would be coming in on the 11th, and I could hear the joy in her voice. We kept telling one another that we could not wait to hug and hold each other because it had been so, so long.

So that night as I went to sleep the feeling that I had was like a child again on at Christmas Eve. I couldn't go to sleep because all I was thinking about was waking up and heading to South Carolina to see my Mary, my early Christmas present!

Seeing, holding, hugging Mary again would be the best Christmas present I could ever hope for and it was coming early! This would be a rendezvous that would be better than either one of us would or could have ever imagined.

Chapter Twenty Seven

The morning of the November the 11th came and it was beautiful. A good day for driving and I could hardly wait to get going. Mom got up and cooked breakfast for me and since I was already packed, all I had to do was load the car and I would be on my way.

After breakfast and saying goodbye to mom and Zoe, I headed out on my way to Hilton Head, South Carolina to see the woman who always had a special place in my heart. My Mary!

I left at approximately eight o'clock and with the time change from Central time zone to Eastern time zone my GPS said that I would arrive around four thirty that afternoon. Man that was a long time I thought. Then I realized that was nothing compared to how long it had been since I had last seen Mary! Eight and a half hours compared to twenty-six years was nothing. I could do those eight and a half hours with one eye closed. I thought better of that because I certainly wanted to make sure that I arrived safely so I could see the love of my life again.

The drive was peaceful and uneventful which was what I was hoping for. Mary had asked me to call her periodically so she would know where I was and to make sure that I was OK, which I did.

When I was about an hour and a half away it started raining slightly and that made the trip slightly longer. I was chomping at the bit to get there, but I made sure that I drove safely as to not have an accident. If it took a few more minutes, that would be OK. What were a few more minutes? Nothing! Nothing at all in the grand scheme of things was what I thought.

When I approached Bluffton, South Carolina, which is right before you cross the bridge to Hilton Head, I noticed the community of Rose Hill and realized that I had just passed where Mary lived. Wow, I thought! I am closer to Mary than I have been in oh so long and that made me a little nervous. Nervous in the fact that I couldn't wait to take Mary into my arms and hold her and to kiss her, if she would let me, like there was no tomorrow.

Funny thing about GPS systems. You would think with the technology that they possess that they would get you to your destination with no problem but sometimes it just doesn't work that way. I am listening to the GPS and it said that I should turn, which I did. I am looking for Mary and there is no Mary to be found, so I decide that I need to call her. I said, "Apparently I'm lost." And told her what I had done. Mary laughed and said that she had made the same mistake, in taking the first entrance instead of the second one on her first trip to the store in Shelter Cove. Mary directed me to keep coming on the street I was on and said, "Turn at the Piggly Wiggly back entrance, then take an immediate right. I will be waiting outside for you."

I was following her instructions and continuing to talk to her as I drove. Then all of a sudden she said, "I see you." My heart skipped as I looked to my right and there she was, MY MARY. She was standing outside waving and smiling at me.

Oh what a beautiful sight she was. After all these years there was Mary. MY MARY was looking at me. I pulled up and rolled down the passenger window, leaned over, and gave her a quick kiss on the lips. The lips that I hadn't kissed for the past twenty-nine years had again finally met mine again. I couldn't wait to park the car and whipped it the first spot that was available.

The car seemed to park itself because all that I was thinking about was grabbing Mary and giving her a hug and not letting go. When I got to where she was standing we hugged one another with such passion that I knew I had to kiss her. Really kiss her this time!

Too many years had passed not to just "lay one on her" and that is what I did. This kiss was definitely longer than the quick peck that we given one another initially and there was something that seemed oh so real. But was it possible? Was I wanting it to be true or was it actually true? What I mean is, when I kissed Mary and she was kissing me back, it seemed oh so right and it seemed that I could feel in my body that Mary "Loved me!" Crazy as it seemed, but I felt that Mary did love me. It was a feeling like no other that I have ever had or at least I hadn't had in a long, long time. This kiss lasted a little longer and since we were in a public place we did not want to make a scene, so we stopped and went inside.

Once inside we begin to talk like we had "never" left each other's side. Mary asked about the trip and said over and over, "Mike you have not changed a bit. You still look the same as you did all those years ago." "Well, thank you, Mary, but I am a lot older and hopefully a lot wiser," was my response. I told Mary that she was just as beautiful as the last time I had seen her at the Memphis Showboat game all those years ago. She laughed and said, "A little plumper, a little more gray and a whole lot wiser." I laughed as well and told her, "You look great, Mary."

We continued to reminisce and talk about what we had been doing, what had happened to the both of us and various other things, but all that I could think about was closing the store and "kissing Mary very, very deeply again and again and again."

Seven o'clock finally rolled around, which seemed to take forever. Kind of like when you are a kid and Christmas Eve has arrived and you cannot wait until it is night time so you can go to bed to awake the next morning to all of the presents Santa brought you the night before.

Christmas had come twice to me in one year and it wasn't even Thanksgiving yet. The first time was when Mary had sent the invite on Facebook and now again, with me standing right in front of the love of my life. I was thinking that if the actual Christmas Day was any better than this, then it would have to be "over the top" because I did not think that it could or would get any better than it was at that moment.

Once all of the paperwork had been completed, the lights turned off, the alarm set and everything locked up I walked Mary to her SUV holding her hand. I felt like I was on a first date and it was still raining slightly. I remember trying to sing "Walking in the Rain with the One I Love" and we headed to her SUV.

When Mary was inside her SUV and I was about to head to my car, Mary grabbed me and we had our first of many passionate kisses. A kiss that said to me, "I have missed you and I am glad that you are here!" This was a total surprise and a great pleasure I might add, in the fact that she could not wait to kiss me again. I felt the same way about kissing her.

The drive to Mary's house seemed like it was taking an eternity, but in all actuality it was probably fifteen to twenty minutes at the most. When we got to where Mary lived, which was a guarded community, which I thought was a great idea for a single woman, we had to stop and get a parking pass for me. This would allow me access in and out while I was visiting.

We pulled up to Mary's home and before we entered Mary said that I needed to take off my hat because she was afraid it would scare Red, the bloodhound. For some reason Red did not like people with hats on so I wanted to make sure that he liked me. Never had been around a bloodhound before and I sure didn't want to piss him off, so off the hat came. Red, the bloodhound, Petey, the lab, and Georgia, the Chihuahua, were in their respective kennels waiting on their mommy to get home to take them outside and feed them.

As I entered the house, Mary let them all out. Since I was new to all of them, they barked at me immediately. It took a few moments but they settled down and we went outside. After they did their business we all went back inside and Mary fed them. I asked if there was anything that I could do and she said, "No Mike. Just relax because I know that you must be tired from driving." Any other time I probably would have been a little tired but seeing Mary again had tripped the adrenaline switch and I was ready to go!

Mary and I went back outside and started to talk. Then I realized there was something that I wanted more than conversation or anything else right then. I wanted to kiss Mary again. I took Mary in my arms and proceeded to kiss her with all of my heart and all of my soul.

This act felt so right that I thought, "This must be a dream." But when I opened my eyes after kissing Mary and she was still in front of me, I knew it was not a dream but a reality. Never in my wildest imagination would I have thought this possible. Only a few months ago, I felt like a ship at sea without a compass. Now here I was with Mary in my arms and loving every second of being with her again. We had been apart all these years, and now we were standing in front of one another and you could just feel the passion rising between the two of us.

We decided to go inside and upon reentry into the house I began to kiss Mary again. After that kiss it was time for a quick tour. She showed me the guest bathroom and then showed me where I could put my travel bag. After this was done she showed me her bedroom and the rest of her home. Before either she or I knew what was happening we were in another passionate embrace. Mary and I were together again, the way we had been, Oh so many years ago. There were no words to express my feelings at that moment. I feel that Mary felt the same way by the way she held me and kissed me back.

Could this actually be happening was what I was asking myself? We had been apart for more than twenty eight years and yet we agreed that it felt like we had never left one another. Was it our kindred spirits searching for something to hold on to because of the tragic events that had entered our lives? Was it the need to feel comfort with someone who had similar feelings in dealing with their loss? What was the connection?

I was the first to say the words that I never thought would ever come from my lips again while I was holding Mary; I looked into her eyes and said, "Mary, I love you! I believe down deep inside of my heart and soul that I never stopped loving you!" Almost immediately and without hesitation said, "And Mike I love you too."

"How can this be happening to us?" was Mary's question to me. "We haven't seen each other in over twenty-six years. We haven't held or kissed one another in twenty-eight years to be exact, and yet I know that I love you, that this feels so natural." I smiled and said, "It must be my bubbly personality." Mary laughed and smiled back and said, "Yeah that's probably what it is, your bubbly personality."

The time that I spent with Mary on my initial reconnecting visit was not long enough. We tried to do as many things as we could before I had to head back to Mississippi. We went for walks on the beach holding hands. We went to dinner together, which may not sound like much, but we were enjoying each other's company, like we were on our first date. We went to an oyster festival, shucked our own oysters, and listened to the bands play on a beautiful Sunday afternoon. We were "a couple" and we were loving every minute of being together again.

Chapter Twenty Eight

While I had been visiting Mary the subject had been broached numerous times on how her children, Riki, Lauren and Kelly, would react if they knew that their mother was in a relationship? Would they be upset? Indifferent? Angry? Hurt? Or elated that their mother had found some happiness? As the old saying goes, "If mother is not happy then no one is going to be happy!" So Mary, as well as I, was hoping that they would understand that their mother needed and wanted to be happy. If I was the person that brought her that happiness, then hopefully they would accept me some day.

Mary was concerned and rightfully so of how they would feel, in that she had been both Mom and Dad to the three of them since Greg's death. There had not been another person in her life except for Greg. Subsequently she had not had to deal with the emotions of bringing a "stranger" into her children's lives. Now she did!

I tried to let Mary know how much I really loved her when I said, "Mary, even though this is the best that I have felt in a long, long, long, time I would never do anything that would make you or your children feel uncomfortable."

What I was trying to say to her was that, "I love you so much that if being with you caused any bad feelings among your kids, then I would step aside." Some people might say, "Well if you really loved her then you would fight for her." To me true love is when a person is willing to sacrifice anything for someone that they love. I would rather go through the pain of losing her again than for her to endure the pain of her children not accepting me. I was willing to do that for Mary but prayed that it would never have to happen.

Mary thought, as I did, that if her kids had a chance to get to know me, they would like me like she did. You never know how kids will react. Hell, they weren't kids, they were adults, and I was sure that this would be much more difficult.

My main objective was to instill in Mary's children that the only reason that I was there with Mary was to make her happy. No other reason whatsoever, just happiness. With that thought and with talking to friends of mine, they were in agreement that if Riki, Lauren, and Kelly spent time around me and their mother seeing that she was happy, then they would accept me a whole lot easier.

Mary and I decided that the sooner I got together with her children, the better, especially if we were going to see where this new reconnection would take us. I agreed because I wanted to be with "My" Mary and I believed that she felt the same way about me.

Chapter Twenty Nine

Monday morning arrived faster than I thought possible, and it was time to get ready to head back to Mississippi. God, I didn't want to leave Mary, but I had to get back to check on my mother and Mary had to go to work. She had a business to run and I had to try and figure everything out that was running through my head.

There was one thing that I knew for sure that needed no thought process whatsoever. If Mary wanted me to come back for another visit, then I would be back! I was hoping she did because I knew in my heart I wanted to be with her more than I thought was possible.

After we got up that morning we were talking trying not to discuss me leaving. We had to really, really concentrate on other things so as to keep our emotions in check. We took the pups out to do their business, had our morning coffee together and talked about how great it had been seeing and being with one another.

I decided it was time to shower and brush my teeth and get packed for the trip back to Mississippi. I wasn't trying to get away in a hurry, but I knew that we were going to be sad the longer I waited to leave. It seemed like I had just gotten to South Carolina and now I was leaving. Man, Oh man, time flies when you are with the "one true love of your life".

Once I was ready I walked up to Mary, took her in my arms, squeezed her tight, and kissed her as passionately as I could. I told her that the time that we had spent together the past few days had been beyond what words could describe. Mary said, "Mike, I have so enjoyed seeing you, being with you again and reconnecting with you. I hope that you will come back to see me again, so we can build on what we have restarted." To which I replied, "Babe, you can count on me coming back because right now I really don't want to leave. I never want to be without you ever again." Mary smiled and said, "Promise?" My reply to that was simple, yet different when I said, "ABSODAMNLUTELY I PROMISE"!

With that I headed out the door to my car, wanting to stop and turn around and stay with "MY" Mary, but I knew that there were several things that would need to happen before we could be together forever. Mary knew that as well and I continued on. We needed to see one another again to make sure that reconnecting was exactly what we both wanted. We needed to get Riki's, Lauren's, and Kelly's blessing as well, if this was to ever work.

As I got in the car I looked back toward the house and thought to myself, "God, you have brought us together again. Why I do not know. I hope that you will give us guidance and be with us as we try to figure out where we are going and how to get there, as a couple."

As I backed out of the drive I waved goodbye not knowing but hoping that Mary could see me and know that she was, has been, and always will be "MY" Mary. That I would see Mary again and hopefully it would be the beginning of a long, happy and loving relationship!

The drive back to Mississippi was long and boring to a certain extent. What I did have was a ton of time to relive what had happened the past few days. I relived everything that Mary and I had done and in doing so, I realized that we were meant to be with one another. Why would two individuals who haven't laid eyes on each other in over twenty-six years, get along so great, if that wasn't the case?

They wouldn't unless this was their destiny! Mary and Mike were supposed to be a couple. Maybe this was supposed to happen many, many years ago and for whatever reason it didn't. Now the former boyfriend, girlfriend, lovers, companions, and best friends had a second chance at love. This Ole Mississippi boy thought during his journey home "I am going to make damn sure that Mary does not get away from me the second time around!"

With that thought I started planning my return trip to see Mary again. Funny thing about that was I had only been gone for less than an hour.

That confirmed to me what I had known since the day that Mary first contacted me. I would do whatever I could to make sure that Mary and I were together for the remainder of our lives, if at all possible. I had decided that I would not pass up the opportunity that I had been given for a second chance at love!

THE END